# Oysters

## A CONNOISSEUR'S GUIDE & COOKBOOK

Recipes By
LONNIE WILLIAMS

Text By
KAREN WARNER

Color Photography By
LISA BLEVINS

Food Styling By
STEVIE BASS

Published In Cooperation With
PACIFIC HEIGHTS BAR & GRILL

101 PRODUCTIONS
San Francisco

## ACKNOWLEDGEMENTS

To Dr. Lawrence Spergel, co-owner Pacific Heights Bar & Grill, for his support and technical assistance.

A special word of thanks to the following food and wine experts for their comments on oysters.
Leon D. Adams, *Wines of America*
M. F. K. Fisher
Phyllis C. Richman, Executive Food Editor, *The Washington Post*
Elaine Tait, Restaurant Critic, *Philadelphia Inquirer*

For their contributions to our oyster tasting guide, our thanks to: the oyster shuckers at Pacific Heights Bar & Grill: Kirk Crist, Georgette Huish, Roger Pence and Tony von Baayer; and also to Mario Staub and Steve Cohen of the Grand Central Oyster Bar in New York City; Bill Marinelli of Marinelli Shellfish; and Nick Mariele of Standard Fisheries Corporation.

And more thanks to:
John Cantu, Anthony Chavez, Dan Coffey, Dan Cohon, Joth Davis, Noreen Eberly, John Finger, Charles Futch, Nancy Granite, Lisa Jang, Shirley and Peter Kowal, Pat La Rocca, Lucy Nichols, Len Pardo, Marsha Polk, Bill Quast, Jorge Rebagliati, Bob Reichenbach, Ed Schwartz, Bill Sieling, Oscar Turner III, Michael Watchorn and Jim Wilson.

*Library of Congress Cataloging-in-Publication Data*

Williams, Lawrence.
   Oysters: a connoisseur's guide & cookbook / Lawrence Williams & Karen Warner.
      p. cm.
   Includes index.
   ISBN 0-89286-281-5     ISBN 0-89286-277-7 (pbk.)
   1. Cookery (Oysters)   2. Oysters.   I. Warner, Karen.   II. Title.
TX754.098W55 1987
641.6′94—dc 19                                          87-13068
                                                            CIP

BOOK DESIGN: Lynne O'Neil

**BLACK AND WHITE PHOTOGRAPHS**
Al Dillow
Jorge Rebagliati
Scott Taylor
Jan Watson
Janice Whipple
State of Florida
   Department of
   Natural Resources

Union Oyster House illustration, Tom Kane

Oysters for photographs provided by Marinelli Shellfish Company

Printed in Singapore by Singapore National Printers Ltd Coordinated by Palace Press.

Distributed to the book trade in the United States by the Macmillan Publishing Company, New York.

Published by
101 PRODUCTIONS
834 Mission Street
San Francisco CA 94103

# Contents

# An oyster shucker's view

"Uh, gimme a half dozen oysters, please." says the man at the bar.

"What kind would you like?" say I. "We have at least twelve different kinds tonight."

The man, hoping things would be simple, squints at the little board bearing names of places he's never been to and can't pronounce.

"How 'bout a half dozen Blue Points?" he says, relieved to find something he could recognize. "I know them."

"Well then, why don't you try something different?" say I. "These Kumamotos are great right now, and they're the same price as the Blue Points."

"Gee, they're so small! Where they from?" says the man.

He's obviously unfamiliar with any oyster not simply called "oysters on the half shell." That's when I'm transformed from "bartender" to "shellfish expert."

I am an oyster shucker. I make my living shucking oysters to be eaten raw on the half shell, a delicacy as mystical as it is delectable. If all I had to do was open oysters, my job would be easy. But it gets more interesting. In addition to shucking, it's my domain to be the resident expert on no less than twenty different kinds of shellfish. Apart from the more mundane information—where they're from and what they taste like—I'm obliged to know how they're grown, what they eat, how they reproduce and, above all, if they are an aphrodisiac.

"Depends on who you are with," I say. "Peanut butter is an aphrodisiac if you're with the right person."

It's funny, as a shucker, one is marine biologist, entertainer, chef and psychotherapist all rolled into one. One minute, I'm explaining the difference between the estuaries of Puget Sound and the Gulf Coast. In my other ear, a woman is asking me what she should do about her indifferent boyfriend. Well, I guess being a jack-of-all-trades *is* a talent. My job wouldn't be so unique if a large percentage of people knew about oysters. But unlike ice cream, many people have not had the opportunity to try different oysters. That's when the element of trust comes in.

To build credibility in recommendation, I need to know where the oysters come from, what time of the year they're best, how they compare with each other and, most importantly, how to suggest how a particular request might be improved. I am an educator with a sharp knife in my hand. The mud on my apron and the occasional swallow of an oyster or two attest to my knowing what I'm talking about. My strange set of circumstances sets me apart from conventional waiter or cook, yet I need to be adept at these jobs too.

"The Kumamotos are of Japanese origin, farmed in Eureka, California. They're medium salty and somewhat creamy in texture with lots of flavor," say I.

"I think I'll stick with the Blue Points," says the man.

At least I tried to knock one soul from the rut. Not that they're bad. But when there's a choice, why not try something new?

Roger Pence, Oyster Shucker
Pacific Heights Bar & Grill

*"You have never
seen the sea,
but in an oyster
on the shell."*

EDMOND ROSTAND
CYRANO DE BERGERAC

7

# Life and times of the oyster

Dr. Science (Dan Coffey) explains it all: "Oysters are actually the thymus glands of whales. When whales mate, the conjugal motion loosens and then releases the thymus glands into the ocean. These then drift on ocean currents, eventually arriving on supermarket shelves. The myth that oysters increase human fertility comes from their origin. Whales are the most passionate of mammal lovers, and even though the whale thymus plays no part in reproduction, it enjoys guilt by association. That's good enough for most sexually insecure humans who have to choose between oysters and rhinoceros horns. At least you can eat an oyster."

Aw shucks, we know that isn't true. An oyster is a member of the *Phylum mollusca* and the class *bivalvia*. Its shell is divided into two halves, not surprisingly called valves. For reasons known only to the oyster, its body lies in the left valve. The valves of the oyster are opened and closed by a powerful adductor muscle that keeps the shell shut to protect it from predators. And it is this muscle that makes shucking an oyster such a challenging job.

The oyster thrives in brackish water, living in bays, coves and estuaries where the currents supply food—plankton and tiny larvae that the oyster strains through its gills. A single oyster can pump one hundred gallons of water through its valves in a day. Thus to keep a bed of oysters fat and content, there must be a great deal of tidal action. Chesapeake, Apalachicola and Tomales bays are all excellent feeding grounds for the oyster.

## THE MYSTERIOUS MOLLUSK MIGRATION

The world's edible oysters belong to two genera: *Ostrea* and *Crassostrea*. That's a pretty simple lesson in marine biology. But the biological history of the oyster becomes quite mysterious when you consider that the *Ostrea* genus is native to Europe and also indigenous to the West Coast of North America, while the Crassostrea

genus has resided along the Atlantic coast of North America and in the waters of Asia for some four thousand years. How did *Ostrea* travel from Europe to California? And how did *Crassostrea* go from Japan to Chesapeake Bay? No one knows.

We do know, however, that during this century *Crassostrea* was imported from Japan to the West Coast, where it thrives. And species of the European *Ostrea* have been cultivated on both coasts of America. *Ostrea* prefers cool and clean water with a sandy bottom surface. The *Crassostrea* oysters are more adaptable to their environment and therefore are more plentiful in North America. They can combat sudden changes in the salinity of the water and excessive sediment. They can live on moderately muddy beds in estuaries, creeks and inlets.

## HER TODAY, GUY TOMORROW

The oyster is a sexy creature and its changeable nature is probably responsible for its reputation. At various stages of an oyster's life it can switch from female to male or from male to female. The oyster can't seem to make up its mind. A number of factors determine the sex of an oyster—the amount of plankton in the diet (a rich food supply encourages the oyster to be female), water temperature, tide and salinity of the water.

The *Crassostrea* oysters usually start off in life as males and after the first year change to females. And if they live long enough, *Crassostrea* may revert back to being male. By contrast, the *Ostrea* oysters change sex continuously. If they live in cold waters, they change their sex once a year during the warm months. *Ostrea* oysters living in warmer waters may change repeatedly from male to female in a single season.

## THE ULTIMATE IN GROUP SEX

Though most of the year the sex of the oyster may be a mystery to the casual observer, there is no doubt during mating season. The male oyster begins the cycle of reproduction by releasing billions of fast-swimming sperm cells into the water. In the *Crassostrea* genus the female oyster responds by giving off millions of free-floating eggs into the sea to be fertilized by the athletic sperm cells.

The female *Ostrea*, on the other hand, lays her eggs inside her shell and opens her valves to take in the male oyster's sperm.

Once a single male starts to spawn it sets off a chain reaction in the oyster bed. All the oysters start discharging eggs and sperm until the waters turn a milky white color. The fertilized eggs develop into larvae that swim about the sea looking for a suitable resting place. Once a comfortable-looking oyster shell or a tree branch is found, the tiny oyster tests the spot with a "foot" that it has grown exclusively for this task. An oyster is particular about choosing a place to set, because once it cements itself to an old shell or a piece of tile, it has made a home for life. An oyster is a sedentary creature, who feels most at home in the company of other oysters. While not prone to move around, the oyster is a sociable chap who lives in beds with millions and millions of others of his own kind.

It is true the oyster's life is a bed of oysters, but it certainly is no bed of roses. A number of predators stalk the oyster: starfish, oyster drills, rays and crabs. These predators find the oyster as fine a dining experience as a customer at a local oyster bar.

> *"There's nothing in Christianity or Buddhism that quite matches the sympathetic unselfishness of an oyster."*
>
> SAKI

SCOTT TAYLOR

*An egret rests on an oyster-covered seawall rock.*

# Four thousand years of oystermania

For thousands of years, cooks and connoisseurs have extolled the culinary virtues of the oyster. The mollusk has inspired Shakespeare to pen metaphors, Ira Gershwin to write lyrics and Casanova to make love. Oysters have graced the tables of Roman emperors, were grown in private parks by French kings and even started a war on Chesapeake Bay. To study the oyster's place in history is to see man at his best, and at his worst.

We will never know for certain who the first person was to enjoy a meal of oysters. Were the oysters on the half shell? Or did this adventurous gourmand throw a dozen shells into a blazing seashore fire? Who can say? We can only speculate about this ancient's delight in discovering the delectable morsel nestled in its protective shell. Some protection! Once the word got out that these plentiful bivalves were just waiting to be plucked from the sea, no shell proved too strong against the oyster's most determined predator—man.

History writers are quick to point out that the ancient Romans and Greeks were noted not only for their conspicuous consumption of oysters, but also for their caring cultivation of the bivalves. Although the Mediterraneans seem to get most of the attention when it comes to historical footnotes on oysters, they weren't the first peoples to discover their culinary value.

More than four thousand years ago the coastal Indians of North America ate oysters in great quantities; vast mounds of shells stand as testimony to the Indians' appetite for the bivalve. Unlike the Romans, who ate tremendous amounts of oysters on the half shell, the American Indian preferred his oysters cooked. In fact, the American Indian is credited with creating the first oyster stew.

Although most history books don't note it, British oyster expert John R. Philpots claimed that long before the Romans and the Greeks took up the practice of cultivating them, artificial oyster

*The American Indian supposedly created the first oyster stew. A contemporary version, served at Pacific Heights Bar and Grill, faces. See recipe, page 79.*

beds existed in China. The Chinese ate their oysters dried and only occasionally would they devour an oyster raw.

From the estuaries of China and from the bays of North America, the oyster was a favorite food in the so-called civilized and uncivilized worlds long before it found favor with the Greek philosophers and the Roman emperors.

## THE GLORY THAT WAS GREECE

Aristotle notes that the early Greeks had a fascination with oysters and actually began to cultivate them as early as the fourth century B.C. Fishermen from Rhodes were aware that young oysters, floating about the water looking for a suitable resting place, would attach themselves to pieces of broken pottery that had settled at the bottom of the sea. The fishermen would encourage the growth of the baby mollusks by tossing pieces of broken dishes on the natural oyster beds. Not only were the fishermen recycling used pottery, a noble deed in itself, but they were also providing a nest for the fledgling oysters.

Greek fishermen took oysters from Pyrrha on the island of Lesbos and moved them to another place in the sea nearby. The oysters thrived in this new location, but failed to reproduce. The Greeks learned a very basic lesson about oyster farming: The place where oysters grow the best is not always where they will reproduce. But the Greeks weren't the only ones who were interested in oyster cultivation.

## THE GRANDEUR THAT WAS ROME

In 95 B.C., Sergius Orata introduced oyster beds to Lake Lucrine, the birthplace of European oyster culture. The method of cultivation was rather simplistic by today's standards. The oysters were taken from their natural beds near the Adriatic Sea and placed in Lake Lucrine until they grew to market size. The oysters that were cultivated in these artificial beds were in great demand at the luxurious tables of Rome. No orgy would be complete without them.

Sergius Orata was not only adept at growing oysters, he was equally gifted at selling his product. He gave his oysters a special name—*calliblephara*—meaning oyster with beautiful eyebrows.

*"The firm Roman
to great Egypt sends
his treasure
of an oyster."*

WILLIAM SHAKESPEARE
ANTONY AND CLEOPATRA

While this may not sound especially appetizing to you, the Romans believed that superior oysters had a fine purple thread that ran around the beard. The oysters with the eyebrows had an edge in the Roman marketplace.

The Roman emperors were well known for their excesses at the dining table. Vitellius was said to have eaten as many as a thousand oysters in a sitting. It's a tossup as to which hurt more—the emperor's stomach from the pains of overindulgence or the slaves' fingers from shucking the hundreds of oysters. The emperor's table reflected the exotic tastes of the times—pickled flamingo tongue and ostrich brains. While these foods taxed the imagination of the Roman chefs, the tiny oyster created havoc in the "transportation services" department of the Roman empire.

No other food made such an incredible journey to satisfy the Roman hungers as did the oysters from France and later from England. The British oyster was first brought to Rome in 78 A.D. in the time of Agrippa. The British oysters were called Rutupian and once they were sampled in Rome they were declared a gastronomical success. Thousands of slaves were employed on the shores of the English Channel, gathering oysters for Roman tables. The oysters were so prized that the Romans paid for them by their weight in gold. The great expense was due to the cost of transportation: The mollusks had to travel by sea and then cross the Alps in snow-covered barrels that kept them alive.

The Romans weren't the only ones who appreciated the oysters from Britain. A tradition dating from 1318 in Colchester, England, is the annual oyster festival celebrated on October 8th, St. Deny's Fair.

## EUROPE ON A HALF SHELL

The Europeans were attuned to the subtle differences in taste and color that the location of the bed brings to an oyster. The oysters in Europe were all the same species, *Ostrea edulis*, but each region produced an oyster that was uniquely its own. For example, the oysters from Marennes, France, have a greenish color to them. The unusual tint so alarmed Mme. de Maintenon that she tried to keep Louis XIV from eating what she thought were poisoned bivalves. The oysters were not in fact tainted; the color was a result of their

## CONSPICUOUS CONSUMPTION

The Roman emperor Vitellius was said to have eaten a thousand oysters at a single sitting. King Henry IV's quota was a paltry four hundred oysters—before dinner! Balzac, on the lower end of the scale, was known to consume as many as one hundred oysters as a prelude to his meal. Every two or three days in turn-of-the-century America, Diamond Jim Brady's favorite restaurant delivered a barrel of Lynnhaven oysters—for his own consumption. In Ireland, they say that in one day a man named Dando ate half his bulk (over two hundred pounds) in oysters. He lived to a ripe old age and when he died, his grave was surrounded with oyster shells.

*America's first cookbook
contained a recipe for oyster
ragout. Ours, facing, adds
scallops to the stew for a
tantalizing appetizer. See
recipe, page 63.*

eating habits. A certain kind of algae is responsible for the green cast of the Marennes.

In 1868, the Fates introduced a new type of oyster to France. A storm forced a Lisbon ship, the *Morlaisien*, to dump her dying oyster cargo off the Bordelais coast. Not all the oysters thrown overboard were dead and soon oystermen in that region were discovering a new kind of oyster: *Crassostrea angulata* or, as they called it, *portugaises*. The new oyster had a rough texture and a cup-shaped shell, unlike the smooth, flat shell of its European cousin. The Portuguese oyster is believed to be the same genus as the Japanese oyster, *Crassostrea gigas*. It is a theory that the Asian oyster came to Portugal, clinging to the ships of the Portuguese explorers. A romantic notion and no doubt true.

Oysters in Europe have a definite season. St. James Day, July 25th, is the first day that oysters legally may be sold in England. As early as the eighteenth century, the English were beginning to realize that their supply of oysters was not inexhaustible. In order to control harvesting, laws were passed placing taxes on underwater lands used for oyster cultivation. By the mid-nineteenth century, the French food writer, Charles Monselet, complained in a letter to a friend: "Oysters seem to be losing ground this year. It can't be more than a breathing spell, a bad joke of fortune." In truth, Europe was running out of oysters.

## WHERE OYSTERS GROW ON TREES

While the Europeans were beginning to realize the vulnerability of *O. edulis*, on the other side of the Atlantic the native Americans were feasting on their own special type of oyster. *C. virginica* was the only oyster species native to the eastern seaboard, with one exception: *C. frons*. The latter attaches itself to the roots of the mangrove trees, which grow on the muddy Atlantic shores from the Carolinas south, and also in the Caribbean. They are called coon oysters because when the mollusk-covered roots are exposed at low tide, raccoons steal the oysters and eat them. Late in the sixteenth century, Sir Walter Raleigh saw the coon oysters growing in Trinidad and became the laughing stock of Queen Elizabeth's court for insisting he saw oysters growing on trees.

After the English ventured toward our shores, a few brave souls

decided to stay. The first permanent English settlement, Jamestown, Virginia, was not without its problems. Due to food shortages in 1610, sixty of the settlers were sent to the mouth of the James River to live on oysters and other seafood. The sea proved bountiful and the wolf was kept from the door. But all things change and oysters, once a staple in the early American diet, became a popular between-meal snack by the nineteenth century.

The Atlantic Coast was rich with oysters, which were both more plentiful and larger than the European variety. When the Dutch purchased Manhattan Island, they also bought Oyster Island which today is known by a different name—Ellis Island. The Indians called Long Island *Sewanahaka*, "Island of Shells."

Although the new land seemed to have a never-ending supply of oysters, the colonists soon learned that was not so. As early as 1715, they were alarmed by the fact that oysters were being overharvested, and in that year passed the first oyster law in America. In essence the law made it illegal for anyone to gather oysters during their spawning season from May to September. Anyone caught violating the law was subject to a twenty-shilling fine. But laws were not enough to control the overharvesting, and, by 1775, the natural beds at Wellfleet on Cape Cod had become practically exhausted.

It was becoming clear that Americans loved oysters as much as their European cousins did. In 1742, William Parks of Williamsburg published the first cookbook printed in America. It was a shortened and most likely pirated version of *The Compleat Housewife* by Eliza Smith, originally published in England in 1727. Parks specified he chose recipes with regard to availability of American produce. Included in the book are recipes for oysters in french rolls and oyster ragout.

## THE ALL-AMERICAN OYSTER

Oysters were becoming as American as oyster pie. It is no coincidence that the country's oldest restaurant still in operation is Boston's Union Oyster House, which began serving oysters in 1826. Daniel Webster frequented its semicircular oyster bar; the great orator would drink brandy and water and eat three dozen oysters at a sitting. The southern plantation owners entertained their guests

*In 1859, residents of New York City spent more money on oysters than on butcher's meat.*

*"A fine purple thread should run 'round the beard, this being looked upon as a sign of superior quality."*

PLINY

*A rare freeze leaves an icy crust on the oysters growing off the coast of North Carolina.*

19

with bushel baskets of freshly dug oysters. Oyster roasts were a popular form of celebrating in the Old South. Biloxi, Mississippi, was famous for its oyster bakes (and streets paved with oyster shells) and Roadanthe, North Carolina, boasted of having the world's largest oyster roast.

The oysters available during the nineteenth century were much larger than those we serve today; they were six to eight inches long. The most famous story concerning the size of American oysters involves British writer William Makepeace Thackeray. While visiting Boston, he was served a half dozen on the half shell. After downing one of the American monsters he commented that he felt "as if I had swallowed a baby."

Oyster cellars were common eateries in the United States during the nineteenth century, offering all you could eat for six cents. At those prices, it's not surprising that New York's Fulton Fish Market sold some fifty thousand oysters daily in 1877. Besides the local oyster cellars, street peddlers did a brisk business keeping up with the increasing demand for oysters.

In the latter half of the nineteenth century, Americans who had never heard the roar of the ocean waters were dining on oysters with some regularity. Trains with oysters packed in barrels of ice delivered their precious cargo to eager diners in Vermont. Storekeepers in Cincinnati kept oysters alive in salt-water tanks. Chicagoans ate oysters that had been shipped first to Ohio, where they were boiled, then sent by rail to the Windy City. In St. Louis, where tons of oysters were shipped up from New Orleans on the Mississippi, batter-fried oysters were a popular after-theater snack.

In 1855, oystermen in New York's East River made a remarkable discovery similar to what the Greeks had learned more than two thousand years ago: Spat (oyster larvae) settle on oyster shells scattered over beds during spawning season. To encourage the oysters' growth, the men began to scatter shells over the beds. That same year the State of New York passed a law to ensure the private oyster farmers the rewards of their labor. Oyster culture was officially endorsed. Moreover, this discovery in the East River took place a full three years before M. Coste, a French scientist known as the father of modern oyster culture, presented the same information to Emperor Napoleon III.

## THE STORY OF TABASCO SAUCE

A veteran of the Mexican-American War brought back some red-pepper seeds to New Orleans. Using these peppers, his friend Edmund McIlhenny developed a hot sauce particularly well suited to oysters. He started marketing it as Tabasco in 1868, well before the Mexican state of Tabasco existed. The formula for the sauce is a well-kept family secret, but Paul C. P. McIlhenny, vice-president of the company today, does share his recipe for saucing half-shell oysters: "One meager drop lemon juice and one meager drop Tabasco pepper sauce."

*Another New Orleans tradition, besides Tabasco Sauce, is the Oyster Loaf or Peacemaker, facing. See recipe, page 74.*

*Oyster lovers gather mol-lusks for their own use at low tide from the natural beds at Horse Island, North Carolina.*

# WAY OUT WEST

While New Yorkers were experimenting in the East River, across the continent Captain J. C. W. Russell of Shoalwater Bay Trade was busy planting oysters in San Francisco Bay. The demand for the indigenous West Coast Olympia oyster during the Gold Rush years had all but exhausted the bay's supply. Russell's goal was to ensure Californians of dining on fresh oysters instead of preserved eastern oysters. But it wasn't until 1896 that the oyster industry took off in San Francisco. M. B. Moraghan received a large order of live eastern oysters and was unable to sell them all in the marketplace. He planted them in the south San Francisco Bay to preserve them for a year. Much to his surprise, the oysters took to their new environment and he started the oyster industry in California. His oysters were served in the fashionable grill rooms of the Palace Hotel.

The popularity of oysters in the nineteenth century gave rise to a new career for some enterprising chaps—oyster pirating. In 1880, Virginia newspapers reported that Chesapeake Bay was crawling with pirates from Baltimore. The pirates, who worked at night, would steal from the privately owned beds. One representative in Virginia's House of Delegates was so outraged he proposed to outfit a steamer vessel manned with sixty men with long-range rifles to protect the oyster beds. Meanwhile in California, Jack London had a brief but glorious career as an oyster pirate, raiding the beds in San Francisco Bay. When he was fifteen, London borrowed three hundred dollars and bought a sloop called the *Razzle Dazzle*. On moonless nights he would raid the oyster beds and sell the stolen goods to saloonkeepers in his hometown of Oakland. London earned more in one night on an oyster raid than he made in three months working twelve hours a day in a local cannery.

By the end of "the oyster century," America was running out of oysters. Massachusetts, Connecticut and New York relied on oysters transplanted to their waters from Chesapeake Bay. Every spring thousands of bushels of oysters were transported north by schooner for the fall and winter markets. By 1880, even Chesapeake Bay could not keep up with local demand, not to mention the increasing demands of the northern markets and the new western markets the continental railroad had created. There were too many people and too few oysters. Overpopulation created other problems

## THE OYSTER IN SAN FRANCISCO

"By the mid 1850s there were oyster merchants in San Francisco, but they apparently depended on the local supply of mainly tiny, but delectable native oysters. Oyster beds were developed in many parts of the bay, particularly close to Sausalito and in Richardson's Bay. By the 1860s there were several popular bars that featured oysters on the half shell and in cocktails. When the transcontinental rail line was first in service, early shipments of Cape Cod and Chesapeake Bay oysters arrived, packed in heavily iced large barrels."

TRAVEL WRITER BOB REICHENBACH, WHO WAS EATING OYSTERS IN SAN FRANCISCO AT THE TURN OF THE CENTURY.

for the oyster industry. As the San Francisco Bay Area became more populated, the bay waters became contaminated. By the early 1920s, only a few cultivated beds remained; the last commercial oysters in San Francisco Bay were harvested in 1936.

## ERSTERS GOT KULCHA

Although the oyster industry was failing in San Francisco Bay, in Washington State experiments with the Japanese seed oyster were just getting underway. *Crassostrea gigas*, the imported Japanese or Pacific oyster, proved to be very adaptable to the waters of the Northwest. The Pacific oyster grew to market size but the North American waters were too cold for the oyster to spawn. Each year seed oysters from Japan had to be imported to supply the oyster beds in Washington. But by a fluke of nature during World War II, a warming trend heated the waters sufficiently to cause the oysters to reproduce. This weather phenomenon saved the Pacific oyster industry during the war years. For many years Pacific oysters were used only for cooking; only in recent times have they become a popular half-shell oyster. Today the wonderful flavor of *C. gigas* has made these oysters bestsellers in West Coast oyster bars.

Although the history of America's culinary love affair with the oyster is charming and in some cases downright amusing, it is not without its consequences. Today from Cape Cod to the Texas-Louisiana Gulf the once-plentiful oyster is petering out. Each year red tides, overharvesting and a multitude of diseases take their toll. Can America be running out of oysters?

Fortunately, conditions are changing. In the past ten years, aquaculturists have given the oyster industry new hope. Oyster farming has become a science. Oyster cultivation carefully nurtures the bivalve through every step of its development—from protecting the larvae in hatcheries to creating new ways for the oyster to develop to maturity, such as using artificial beds made of wooden racks and plastic bags. This new group of marine-life pioneers is proving that the oyster industry can once again be a major force in the seafood market.

*The oysters in San Francisco Bay were killed off by a great earthquake in 1868. Their death was attributed to the heating of the bay bottom resulting from the quake.*

*A favorite food of the forty-niners, which found its way to San Francisco, is Hang-town Fry, facing. See recipe, page 78.*

25

# Life is a bed of oysters

Oysters have been cultivated for thousands of years. The Chinese and Romans were experimenting with new ways to grow oysters before the birth of Christ. But the development of more sophisticated methods of cultivation has been slow in coming. Why should we learn how to grow oysters more efficiently when we have an inexhaustible supply on our coastline? Gradually, in some parts of North America, this attitude has been changing. Today, each region has its own laws and regulations governing the growth and harvesting of oysters. The laws are as varied as the rugged coast of New England is different from the sandy beaches of Texas.

## REAPING THE NATURAL BED

In the eastern United States, most of the oysters are grown in natural beds, rather than cultivated, and harvested by two traditional methods: Tonging is the more ecologically sound method, while dredging is more commercially efficient.

Tongs are hinged wooden poles that can be as long as twenty-six feet; at the end are two baskets equipped with teeth. The oysterman, or woman, stands in a boat and plunges the tongs into the water until they hit the oyster reef. The fisherman works the tongs like a pair of scissors, forcing the handles together which causes the teeth to scoop the oysters into the baskets. The catch is hoisted onto the boat and the process is repeated. Tonged oysters are sorted or culled by the oysterman, who returns undersized oysters and dead shells to the bed.

A dredge has a boxlike metal frame about six feet wide and, in front, a blade that loosens the oysters from the bed. The box acts as a scraper, scooping the mollusks into a metal bag attached to the frame. A dredge can scoop up a thousand or more oysters at a time, but the harvest is seldom culled to discard shells or return small oysters to the reef.

*What could be more American than Corn Fritters and Oysters? Photo faces. See recipe, page 64.*

26

*A skipjack dredges oysters on Chesapeake Bay.*

Although there are some similarities in the methods used to harvest oysters, the techniques for growing oysters and regulations concerning their harvest are rapidly changing in many regions of the country. Space does not permit a detailed account of all the major oyster-producing regions of the United States and Canada. We present here only a representative sampling of the various geographic areas to give an overview of the traditional and contemporary methods of cultivation, as well as some of the issues that environmentalists are dealing with today.

## COTUIT: GRANDDADDY OF CAPE COD

Founded in 1837, the Cotuit Oyster Company is the oldest brand name of oysters in the United States and the largest commercial operation in Cape Cod. Massachusetts leases its bay-bottom land to encourage oyster cultivation. At Cotuit Oyster Company, seed oysters are purchased from a Long Island hatchery and transferred into surface trays that are submerged in the bay waters. Once the seed oysters are about an inch in size, they are placed onto the oyster bed in the bay bottom for the final grow-out process. In recent years, production of the Cotuit oyster has been below par; the MSX organism has destroyed much of Cape Cod's oyster crop.

## OYSTER WARS ON CHESAPEAKE BAY

The heart of the oyster industry in the United States is Chesapeake Bay. To understand the current method of cultivation here, it is necessary to know a little of the history. In the 1880s the bay was producing fifteen million bushels of oysters each season, from mid-September through March. During this era, a new invention, the dredge, was replacing tongs as a more effective, and more devastating, instrument used to harvest oysters. The dredge was depleting the New England beds with a sinister efficiency. To prevent Chesapeake Bay from being raped by the power dredge, the Maryland legislature enacted laws making it illegal to harvest oysters except under sail. In the same spirit of conservation, Maryland also passed a cull law requiring oystermen to sort through their catch and return any undersized or dead shells to the reef, thus ensuring a substantial bed for new growth.

A. DILLOW

While Maryland was enacting legislation to preserve natural oyster production, Chesapeake Bay was becoming a battleground. Fierce competition between the sail dredgers and the tongers sparked violent conflicts that often ended in bloodshed. Though a special oyster navy was formed to police the waters, the oyster wars went on until World War I. Finally, a legal compromise was reached and Chesapeake Bay was open to both tonging and sail dredging, but the tributaries, with the exception of Choptank Bay, were reserved for tongers only.

Today sail-powered skipjacks still work Chesapeake Bay for oysters, but a law passed in the 1950s makes it legal for powerboats to dredge the bay on Mondays and Tuesdays. Ninety percent of the oystering in Maryland is on public land and there is strong public sentiment to keep it that way. Though a small portion of the bay bottom is leased, law prohibits leasing land that has natural oyster beds. The state hopes to encourage aquaculture activity on the leased land. According to Maryland's natural resource manager, Bill Sieling, drought conditions in recent years have caused the salinity levels in Chesapeake Bay to rise, making a natural breeding ground for oyster diseases. The oysters reproduce and live well in the saltier waters, but they are more vulnerable to salt-loving parasites. These conditions have reduced oyster production dramatically; the 1986–87 harvest was under a million bushels.

## WHERE HAVE ALL THE BLUE POINTS GONE?

In Long Island, home of the internationally known Blue Point, wild oyster beds were plentiful at the turn of the century. Over a thousand commercial oyster fishermen worked in Long Island during the 1920s. Today only one commercial oyster business remains in the area. In the 1950s, overpopulation of the Oyster Bay area caused the waters to become polluted. Fortunately, in recent years the waters have greatly improved.

The sole survivor of the oyster industry in Long Island, Flowers Oyster Company, has a hatchery in Bayville, New York. Here the oysters spawn and the tiny larvae are put in tanks where they attach themselves to crushed oyster shells. After a couple of months, the seed oysters are large enough to be spread on trays and suspended from floating rafts in Oyster Bay. Once the babies reach

THE CARE AND FEEDING OF OYSTERS as explained in *Housekeeping in Old Virginia* (1877): "Mix one pint of salt with thirty pints of water. Put the oysters in a tub that will not leak, with their mouths upwards, and feed them with the above, by dipping in a broom and frequently passing over their mouths. It is said that they will fatten still more by mixing fine meal with the water."

*In Virginia, and other parts of the south, Oyster Pie (facing page) is a traditional dish with holiday turkey or ham. For our version, see recipe on page 74.*

a size of about two inches, they are planted onto a prepared bed. After about two years, they have reached maturity and are ready to harvest for market. With the development of increased scientific knowledge, perhaps more oyster hatcheries will be opened in the Long Island area.

## SON OF THE SUN BELT

According to Charles Futch, assistant director of Florida's Division of Marine Resources, 90 percent of the state's commercial oyster crop is grown in Apalachicola Bay. Florida issues few bay-bottom leases and most of its oysters are grown and harvested on public land. For twenty-five dollars, anyone in Florida can buy a permit to harvest oysters in the publicly owned beds. Since the low cost of a commercial permit opens the doors for some pretty stiff competition, Florida law allows oysters to be harvested by the tong method only. In order to protect the last stronghold of the oyster industry in Florida, the state has purchased land surrounding Apalachicola Bay to keep the waters pollution free. Like many of the Sun Belt states, Florida is growing at a phenomenal rate—nine hundred new

*"The eldest Oyster winked his eye, And shook his heavy head. Meaning to say he did not choose To leave the oyster bed."*

LEWIS CARROLL
THROUGH THE LOOKING
GLASS

*Tonging for oysters in Florida.*

FLORIDA CONSERVATION NEWS

residents per week. With such dramatic increases in population, it is not surprising that many of the state's most productive oyster beds have become contaminated and are no longer safe for growing shellfish.

Despite the depletion of oyster production over the years, Florida is proud of her oysters. Each year shellfish lovers celebrate at an annual seafood festival in Apalachicola, which has hosted oyster-eating and shucking contests for the past twenty years.

## ARE THEY BIGGER AND BETTER IN TEXAS?

Another region that's proud of its oysters is Texas. As in Florida, most of Texas's commercial oysters are grown on state-owned bay bottom. Leases are granted, but leased bay bottom must either be oyster free or not have a natural reef that has produced oysters in the past seven years. The idea of the Texas law is to stimulate aquaculture to create new oyster beds in the gulf, but this has not been accomplished. The leased lands, for the most part, are being used as oyster parks where oysters are transplanted from contaminated waters to live until they are healthy enough for the market.

Most of Texas's oyster crop comes from wild oyster beds. But, unlike Florida, Texas allows dredging in publicly owned oyster reefs. Although a boat may operate only one dredge at a time with a maximum capacity of two barrels, it is easy to see that the Texas oyster beds are quickly becoming depleted.

## CULTURE COMES TO THE WILD WEST

In North America the overwhelming majority of oysters are still grown on bay-bottom beds that occur naturally. But on the West Coast more and more oyster beds are being cultivated, using the latest discoveries in aquaculture. The Japanese or Pacific oyster (*C. gigas*) has been grown on the West Coast since the early 1920s. In Washington, where the Pacific oyster was first introduced to America, growers have been experimenting with methods of cultivating oysters for over sixty years.

The Japanese developed a "hanging cultch" method of growing oysters. Fishermen place bamboo sticks in the water with oyster shells attached to them or ropes with shells hanging from them.

The oyster larvae attach themselves to the shells. This hanging method of growing oysters not only protects them from predators, but also makes harvesting an easier process: The poles or ropes are simply raised from the water. The Japanese method has had a great influence on oyster farmers on the West Coast.

## HIGH-TECH ON THE CALIFORNIA COAST

In Tomales Bay, just north of San Francisco, aquaculturists are utilizing the latest oyster technology. In the late 1970s a new method of cultivating oysters was introduced. Instead of using whole oyster shells to catch the larvae, farmers began using tiny pieces of ground shells. The results are impressive. This method produces a much higher proportion of single-shell oysters, desirable for the half-shell trade. Since most oysters don't reproduce in Tomales Bay, seed oysters are developed in hatcheries.

The next step in development is to place the seed oysters in bags or fine-wire-screen trays suspended in the water. The oysters are kept in the floating nurseries until they are about an inch long and are periodically sorted to ensure uniform size. Now the oyster is ready to grow to market size. Some farmers grow their oysters to maturity on the bay bottom until they are harvested. But the off-bottom technique, with several different harvesting methods, is a far more sophisticated way to nurture the maturing crop. A new breed of aquaculturist working in Tomales Bay is developing additional methods, each unique, for maturing the bivalves off the bay bottom.

John Finger and Michael Watchorn farm their Sweetwater and Kumamoto oysters in the north end of Tomales Bay near Hog Island, which lends its name to their small company. John and Michael raise their seed oysters in water-suspended trays until they reach about an inch in size. Then the infant mollusks are transferred into heavy plastic mesh bags that resemble giant Brillo pads. The bags are tied to metal racks that keep the oysters off the muddy bay bottom until they reach market size.

Next to Hog Island's farm is Lisa Jang's and Jorge Rebagliati's Bay Bottom Beds. The name is deceiving since their oysters never touch the bottom of Tomales Bay. Lisa and Jorge have developed a

## ON BEING AN OYSTER FARMER

Perhaps the best part of the business is the environment necessary to sustain it. There is nothing quite like going out on Tomales Bay late in spring when the low tides are in the early morning. The water is glass calm; the only sounds come from the foraging sea birds. As the sun rises, the fog recedes. The tide turns and once again begins to fill the bay. It all seems so well orchestrated, another cycle beginning.

JOHN FINGER
HOG ISLAND OYSTER
COMPANY

*Cioppino, facing, was created by the Italian fishermen in San Francisco. See recipe, page 83.*

*In Tomales Bay, California, aquaculturists utilize the latest oyster technology. Right, stacks of trays are beneath Bay Bottom Beds' innovative intertidal longline. And during low tide at Hog Island, below, the mesh bags of oysters may be easily removed from their racks.*

unique system for maturing their seed oysters. They place the tiny oysters in trays that are stacked one atop the other and suspended in water by a Styrofoam flotation device. The floating trays are moored to poles with a mother line. Lisa and Jorge have christened their method the "Intertidal Longline Tray Culture," and claim this technique keeps their oysters cleaner because silt doesn't accumulate. The main advantage to this method is that the farmers don't have to wait for low tide to work with their oysters. They can have access to their crop at any time.

Tomales Bay Oyster Company, located in the southern end of the bay, is the oldest continuously operating oyster company in California, dating back to 1907. Back in the 1850s, eastern oysters were imported via the transcontinental railroad to the site of the Tomales Bay farm. The Wellfleets and Blue Points were held in Tomales Bay until they revived from their long journey across country. Then they were sold in the Gold Rush town just south of Tomales Bay—San Francisco.

Today Tomales Bay Oyster Company produces a distinctive-looking Pacific oyster with a deep cup and a rich brown color. Like Hog Island, Tomales Bay buys seed oysters and raises them in a submerged rack until the oyster reaches about one inch in size. The small oysters are then transferred into expandable plastic mesh bags. These are hung on long fiberglass poles in the bay's intertidal zone, where at low tide the oysters are exposed to the air from two to six hours. The oysters grow to full maturity in the bags.

Tomales Bay's farm manager, Jim Wilson, began using the "stick and bag" technique at the farm about two years ago. He borrowed the method from researchers in Washington state and adapted it to the needs of his farm. This method of cultivation creates a deep-cupped oyster that has a tightly sealed top, making the mollusk ideal for shipping. Its unique dark-brown coloring is caused by the algae that grow in the farmed waters of Tomales Bay.

## PACESETTERS OF THE PACIFIC NORTHWEST

Laws passed in Washington in the 1890s provided for bay-bottom lands to be privately owned as well as leased, measures that have allowed aquaculture to flourish. Additionally, however, oysters grow

## THE UTILITARIAN OYSTER SHELL

In ancient Rome, a cement was made from figs, pitch and powdered oyster shells. During the same era, powdered cuttlefish bones and oyster shells were used to cure wounds and ulcers. In sixteenth-century France, during the siege of La Rochelle, the Huguenots used oysters as projectiles after their ammunition ran out. Later, in the New World, the Spanish fort at Pascagoula, Mississippi, was built with moss-mud and oyster-shell walls. So what to do with oyster shells today? Use them as Christmas tree ornaments, or fill a clear glass bowl with the shells for a table centerpiece. Or collect the tiny Kumamoto or Olympia shells and make wonderful earrings.

wild in public areas of certain Washington bays. These reefs are protected by conservation laws that specify how these oysters are to be harvested: They must be picked by hand, they must be shucked on the beach and the shells must be returned to the location where the oysters were found. The shells make a base on which a new crop of oysters can grow.

Experiments with a new triploid oyster are under way at the University of Washington. Under the direction of Dr. Kenneth Chew, Stan Allen and Sandra Downing have developed an oyster that has three chromosomes, instead of the normal two. The triploid oyster does not spawn at all and thus has a consistent flavor throughout the year. While the implications of this work are encouraging to the oyster industry, the results of the experimentation remain mixed. Once the oysters have been chemically treated, there is no way to predict what percentage of the crop will become true triploids. Test results range from as low as 35 percent to as high as 92 percent. Until a predictably large percentage of the treated oysters become triploid, the economic advantages of this process remain in question. The triploid oysters are available commercially from both Westcott Bay Oysters and Coast Oyster Company in Washington.

While oyster farming is flourishing on the West Coast, the rest of North America's oyster industry is waging a war against disease, pollution and overharvesting. Oysters are a gift of nature and should be protected. A case can be made to encourage more states to enact legislation providing for more bay bottom to be leased for aquaculture. Creativity in shellfish production abounds in the Northwest, where private leases and ownership of bay bottom are permitted. Stronger conservation laws are needed to ensure healthy waters that provide a breeding ground for oysters. Let's hope that future generations will be able to enjoy the sea's bounty.

*"Olympia oysters, served at Olympia, are the most delicate I've ever tasted."*

LEON D. ADAMS

*A trio of tempting appetizers faces: (clockwise from bottom) Broiled Oysters with Bacon and Shallots (page 57), Barbecued Oysters Pacific Heights Style (page 57) and Oyster Ceviche (page 55).*

# Shucking oyster mythology

## CAST YE YOUR PEARLS

Poets have waxed eloquent about the pearl and the oyster. Song-writers have written lyrics that show off new ways to rhyme oyster and pearl. For years people have been eating oysters hoping to find a pearl hiding in the half shell. The truth is that neither William Shakespeare nor Ira Gershwin ever found a pearl in his Whitstable or Wellfleet. Pearls do not grow in oysters. This may sound like heresy, but it is simple fact.

The pearl-producing mollusk, *Meleagrina margaritifera*, is not an oyster at all, but more closely related to the mussel. Mother-of-pearl (nacre), the iridescent substance that gives the pearl its lustre, is found inside its shell. It's true that an oyster (or any mollusk), when irritated by a foreign substance in its shell, will form an object resembling a pearl. But an oyster does not produce the nacre necessary to give a pearl its luminescence.

## JURNE, JURLY AND ARGUST

Another myth about oysters, which persists through the years, is that they should not be eaten in months that do not have the letter "R" in their name. No doubt there was a time when there was some basis for this belief. Before modern refrigeration, it was difficult to transport oysters in the summer months. More significantly, during summer months, when the oyster reproduces, its meat is at first fat and gooey, later lean and watery, but in no way harmful to eat. (Oysters are at their flavor peak when they are not reproducing.) In some areas, in order to protect the oyster crop from overharvesting, laws made it illegal to gather oysters during their reproductive months. Perhaps a misinformed public assumed the law meant that oysters were dangerous to eat during that time of year.

While it is true that you will never find a pearl in your Kumamoto, console yourself by knowing that you safely can enjoy a cool glass of champagne and a dozen oysters on the half shell on a sultry summer afternoon.

## APHRODITE ON THE HALF SHELL

How did oysters get the reputation for being an aphrodisiac? No self-respecting Roman orgy would be complete without a Nubian slave shucking thousands of oysters to satiate the lusty diners. History's greatest lover, Casanova, credited the oyster with enhancing his legendary prowess in the boudoir. And in more recent times, the Oyster Institute of America adopted as its slogan: "Eat Oysters, Love Longer." Deserved or not, the oyster has maintained a timeless mystique when it comes to passion.

Actually, any food from the sea can be thought of as possessing the qualities that enhance amour. The sea and romance will be forever intertwined because Aphrodite, the goddess of love, rose from the deep with the power of granting beauty and invincible charm to others. The Fates had assigned Aphrodite the divine duty to make love (nice work if you can get it). And there is something about that salt water. It became a popular notion that those who ate the most seafood were the most fervent in love. Who are we to dispute such a wonderful idea? To test it out, drink the oyster liquor in your half shell—it's all sea water.

Besides the myth, there may be some substance and scientific basis for believing seafood can be an enhancement to love. Phosphorus, iron, copper and iodine (minerals and elements that are plentiful in seafood) are believed to contribute to the efficiency of the sex glands. Some claim that Vitamin D increases our sexual desire and oysters provide a rich source for this vitamin.

The debate wages on whether there really is such a thing as a true aphrodisiac. We will probably never know for sure. But next time you are out to dinner, take note of the number of couples holding hands and stealing kisses while finishing off a dozen oysters on the half shell. Judge for yourself.

*In Wales it was believed that pale young women would improve if they were fed oysters. And on the other side of the world, the Chinese believed that oysters cure freckles.*

41

# A connoisseur's guide to oysters

Oysters and wine not only complement each other as a fine dining experience. They share another characteristic: subtle variations in color, flavor and texture. For example, take a cutting from a Zinfandel vine and plant it in a different region; the grapes produced will take on their own distinctive flavor. Sunlight, rainfall and soil conditions all play a part in creating a wine's character.

Similarly, oysters of the same species take on a subtle and sometimes not-so-subtle difference when grown in different beds. The action of tides, salinity of water, availability of food and presence of algae are all contributing factors that cause the variance of an oyster's shape, color and flavor.

The Roman emperors, who so highly prized the oysters from Brittany, were coveting the same species that grew in their own waters—*Ostrea edulis*. Both Nero and, a few centuries later, Diamond Jim Brady claimed they could identify an oyster's origin blindfolded.

Four species of oysters are commercially cultivated in North America. The two most prevalent are *Crassostrea virginica* (the native Atlantic and Gulf oyster) and *Crassostrea gigas* (the Pacific oyster transplanted from Japan). The other species are *Ostrea lurida*, the highly prized tiny Olympia, indigenous to the Pacific Northwest, and *Ostrea edulis* (sold as Belon), the oyster native to Europe that is now grown in Maine and the Northwest.

Each of these oysters has characteristics common to its particular species. But, like fine wine, oysters have unique differences derived from the locale where they are grown.

We have compiled a guide that lists the oysters by their commercial names as they are identified in oyster bars, restaurants and seafood markets. The guide, by no means complete, is meant to enhance your knowledge and also your enjoyment of oysters.

*The connoisseurs gather at Pacific Heights Bar & Grill.*

# SPECIES OF OYSTERS IN NORTH AMERICA

## CRASSOSTREA GIGAS

Pacific oyster, indigenous to Japan, widely grown in California and Pacific Northwest. Oblong shaped with a deep ridged cup. More strongly flavored than Atlantic and Gulf oysters.

## CRASSOSTREA VIRGINICA

Indigenous oyster to the Atlantic Coast and Gulf states. Shells range from round and flat on the Atlantic oysters to oblong and deep cupped on the Gulf varieties. Generally mild.

## OSTREA LURIDA

The only indigenous West Coast oyster (Olympia), now grown in the Pacific Northwest. The smallest commercially grown oyster, with a tiny, round, flat shell.

## OSTREA EDULIS

A European oyster now cultivated in New England and the Pacific Northwest. It has a craggy, round shell, and a mild, sweet flavor.

# A SELECTION OF OYSTERS OF NORTH AMERICA

## ALABAMA GULF

*Crassostrea virginica*
Bayou La Batre and Mobile Bay. Medium size, mild and meaty.

## APALACHICOLA

*Crassostrea virginica*
Apalachicola Bay, Florida. Medium size with a round, pointed green shell and a large cup. Firm with a mild, slightly sweet flavor.

## BELON

*Ostrea edulis*
The oyster of Brittany is now grown on both coasts of North America. Those from Maine and New Hampshire are larger and more strongly flavored than those grown in California. Both have round, flat shells and a pronounced metallic flavor.

## BLACK BAY

*Crassostrea virginica*
Black Bay, Louisiana. Varying in size and shape: small to large, round to oblong. Mild and sweet with a musky, almost spinachlike aftertaste.

## BLUEPOINT

*Crassostrea virginica*
Originally from Blue Point, Long Island, but is no longer harvested. Bluepoint is now a generic term for mild Atlantic oysters.

## BRAS D'OR

*Crassostrea virginica*
Cape Breton, Nova Scotia. Grown wild, these oysters have flat bodies and curved shells. Their flavor is sweeter and less salty than a Malpeque.

## BRISTOL

*Crassostrea virginica*
South Bristol, Maine. Small to medium size with a round shell and plump body. Flavor is fairly salty and gamey.

## CHESAPEAKE BAY

*Crassostrea virginica*
Chesapeake Bay, Maryland and Virginia. Small to medium size with a mild, sweet flavor. Round shell with a small cup.

## CHINCOTEAGUE

*Crassostrea virginica*
Chincoteague Bay, Maryland and Virginia. Small to medium with a flat, round shell. Sweet with distinctive aftertaste.

## COTUIT

*Crassostrea virginica*
Cotuit Harbor, Cape Cod, Massachusetts. Medium to large with a plump body and fairly salty flavor.

## EMERALD POINT

*Crassostrea virginica*
Emerald Point Bay, Mississippi. A small, mild, creamy oyster.

## FLORIDA GULF

*Crassostrea virginica*
Horseshoe Beach and Wakulla Bay, Florida. Small to medium with an oblong shell. Firm and creamy with a mild ocean flavor.

## GOLDEN MANTLE

*Crassostrea gigas*
Vancouver, British Columbia. Small with a golden color and a beautiful white ridged shell. The delicate flavor is like watermelon with a clean aftertaste.

## HOG ISLAND SWEETWATER

*Crassostrea gigas*
Tomales Bay, California. Small to medium with a fluted, deep-cupped shell. Plump and creamy with a sweet, smoky flavor.

## INDIAN RIVER
*Crassostrea virginica*
Cape Canaveral on the Atlantic coast of Florida. Small to medium with a deep cup and a zesty ocean flavor.

## JAMES RIVER
*Crassostrea virginica*
James River, Virginia. Medium size, creamy and sweet with a hint of salt.

## KENT ISLAND
*Crassostrea virginica*
Kent Island, Chesapeake Bay, Maryland. Medium-size oval shell, plump body and a clean flavor.

## KUMAMOTO
*Crassostrea gigas*
Washington State; Tomales Bay and Humboldt Bay, California. Smallest of the Pacific oysters with a deep-cupped, ridged shell. Creamy and plump with a mild, fruity flavor.

## LOUISIANA GULF
*Crassostrea virginica*
Harvested in the bayous of the Mississippi delta. Thick shell and very plump meat with a soft fatty texture. Slightly salty with a trace of metallic flavor.

## MALPEQUE
*Crassostrea virginica*
Prince Edward Island, Canada. Small with a slightly bitter, lettucelike flavor, clean aftertaste and firm, juicy texture. Pointed oblong shell.

## NELSON BAY
*Crassostrea virginica*
Nelson Bay, Alabama. Medium to large with a very mild, not salty, but slightly fishy flavor. Plump and meaty with a round, flat shell.

## OLYMPIA
*Ostrea lurida*
Puget Sound, Washington, and Humboldt Bay, California. The smallest North American oyster, originally grew wild from Alaska to California. The tiny shell is round and flat. Robust flavor with a mild coppery aftertaste.

## PORTUGUESE
*Crassostrea gigas*
Vancouver, British Columbia. Small to large with a green ruffled shell, deep cup and rounded top. Plump and juicy with a clean, strong ocean flavor. This is not the true Portuguese species *C. angulata*.

## PRESTON POINT
*Crassostrea gigas*
Tomales Bay, California. Small to medium, tiger-striped shell. Creamy with a melony aftertaste.

## QUILCENE
*Crassostrea gigas*
Quilcene Bay, Washington. Fairly briny, with a cucumberlike flavor and strong aftertaste.

## RHODE ISLAND SELECT
*Crassostrea virginica*
Southeast Rhode Island coast. Meaty with crisp flavor.

## ROCK POINT
*Crassostrea gigas*
Dabob Bay, Puget Sound, Washington. A small oyster with a fruity, mildly salty flavor and a coppery aftertaste.

## SKOKOMISH
*Crassostrea gigas*
Hood River, Washington. Medium size with a round shell and sweet cucumbery flavor.

## TEXAS GULF
*Crassostrea virginica*
Galveston Bay and Corpus Christi, Texas. Very meaty and mild, saltier than Louisiana Gulf.

## TOMALES BAY
*Crassostrea gigas*
Tomales Bay, California. Firm, plump, medium size with a deep cup and a beautiful black ruffled shell. Medium-strong, briny, crisp, clean flavor.

## WELLFLEET
*Crassostrea virginica*
Cape Cod, Massachusetts. Small to medium size with an oval shell, moderately salty, clean flavor.

## WESCOTT BAY
*Crassostrea gigas*
Wescott Bay and Tiger Bay, Washington. Pinkish-white, medium-size shell with a deep cup. The flavor is salty with a coppery aftertaste.

## WILLAPA BAY
*Crassostrea gigas*
Willapa Bay, Washington. Plump, medium size with a deep cup and multicolored shell. Flavor is medium salty, clean and sweet.

## YAQUINA BAY
*Crassostrea gigas*
Yaquina Bay, Oregon. Medium size with an oblong, craggy chalk-white shell. Creamy, firm texture and a mild flavor.

# A cook's guide to oysters

## TIPS ON BUYING OYSTERS

• Purchase oysters from a reputable seafood dealer
• Oyster shells should be tightly closed. If a shell is slightly agape, tap the shell with a knife. The shell should close; discard any that do not.
• Freshly shucked oysters have a sea-breeze odor.
• The liquor of a freshly shucked oyster will be a clear, slightly milky or light gray liquid that surrounds the meat.

### HOW MUCH TO BUY
*For each person*

Oysters shucked: ¼ pint
Oysters in the shell: 6 (½ dozen)
Oysters breaded: 4 to 6 pieces

### TESTING FOR FRESHNESS

If the oyster is alive and fresh, the shell will be closed tightly and will not open easily. A simple test will tell you if you have a fresh oyster: Simply tap the shell; a live oyster will close tightly to protect itself and it is fit to eat. The opposite holds true when testing the freshness of a cooked oyster: If the shell stays closed after cooking, the oyster is probably not fresh and should be tossed out.

### GRADING OF SHUCKED PACIFIC OYSTERS
(*Crassostrea gigas*)

*Large:* less than 8 oysters per pint
*Medium:* 8 to 12 oysters per pint
*Small:* 12 to 18 oysters per pint
*Extra small:* more than 18 per pint

### GRADING OF SHUCKED ATLANTIC AND GULF OYSTERS
(*Crassostrea virginica*)

*Extra Large or Counts:* less than 20 per pint
*Large or Extra Select:* 20 to 26 per pint
*Medium or Select:* 26 to 38 per pint
*Small or Standard:* 38 to 63 per pint
*Very Small:* more than 63 per pint

## NOW THAT I'VE GOT THE OYSTER HOME, WHAT DO I DO WITH IT?

### STORING OYSTERS IN THE REFRIGERATOR

• Store shucked oysters in a leakproof bag or in a covered jar. Freshly shucked oysters have a shelf life of 5 to 7 days.

- Store live oysters in a shallow dish covered with damp cloth or paper towels. Never put live oysters in water or in an airtight container, where they would suffocate and die.
- Oysters in the shell are to be used within 7 to 10 days. Some oysters may open their shells during storage. If so tap them: They will close if alive; if not discard.
- After purchasing oysters the shells will probably need to be cleaned. Scrub the oyster thoroughly using a brush under cold tap water.

### FREEZING FRESH OYSTERS

Scrub oysters thoroughly, removing all mud and grit. Remove oysters from their shells using one of the following shucking techniques. Reserve the oyster liquor. Wash oysters in cold salted water, drain and pack in an airtight container. Cover with the oyster liquor, leaving room for expansion, seal and freeze.

Frozen oysters will keep up to one month. Thawed oysters are not suitable for the half shell; they are best in soups, stews and sauces.

## HOW TO SHUCK AN OYSTER

There are several ways to open an oyster and with a little practice you can become skilled at the art of shucking. With all, however, you will need a good oyster knife.

We offer you three basic methods for opening oysters. The first technique is used by professional shuckers and may take intense concentration, not to mention lots of practice on the part of the novice. But once you master this method, you will be the toast of the next holiday dinner, when oysters on the half shell are a must.

The second method requires more paraphernalia (a small hammer and a block on which to rest the oysters), but less skill on the part of the shucker. And the third method requires the intervention of technology—a microwave oven (or, as an alternative, a regular oven).

## REFLECTIONS OF AN OYSTER SHUCKER

I like to offer my customers a variety of different types of oysters and try to get them to eat the oysters without any horseradish or cocktail sauce. That way they can really taste how each oyster is different. While they're eating, I tell them how each oyster is unique. I talk about flavor, size, saltiness and so on. I like to wait on the inexperienced oyster eaters and dispel any shellfish phobias they may have. I guess the most important part of my job is answering questions: "How can you tell them apart?" "Why do you tap the oyster?" "Is that a baby?" "Do the little ones taste sweeter?"

TONY VON BAAYER
OYSTER SHUCKER
PACIFIC HEIGHTS BAR & GRILL

### SHUCKING METHOD I

1) Scrub oyster to get rid of any mud or grit.

2) Protect your hand by wearing heavy-duty rubber gloves or enclose oyster in several thicknesses of a folded kitchen towel. Hold the shell in the palm of your hand with the left valve, the deeper side, down.

3) Locate the beak (the hinged part of the oyster—the narrow end), and with a back-and-forth motion gently work the tip of the oyster knife between the shell halves.

4) Once the knife has penetrated the shell (by ¼ inch or so) make sure the oyster is firmly impaled on the blade by giving the shell a few shakes. It should remain firmly stuck on the end of the knife. Working very carefully, twist the knife back and forth to open the shell.

5) Once the shell is opened, slide the knife across the top of the shell to cut the adductor muscle and run the knife under the body of the oyster. Discard the top shell.

### SHUCKING METHOD II

1) Scrub oyster to get rid of any mud or grit.

2) Wearing gloves to protect your hands (or using a folded towel) place oyster on a block (deep side of the oyster down) with the bill (thin end) of the oyster extending outward. With a small hammer break the shell.

3) Insert the blade of the oyster knife between the shells and cut the adductor muscle at the top of the shell. Pry the top of the shell off, using the blade as a lever.

4) Cut the muscle away from the lower shell by running the blade under the oyster's body.

*"Why, when the world's mine oyster, which I with sword will open."*

WILLIAM SHAKESPEARE
THE MERRY WIVES
OF WINDSOR

### THE MICROWAVE METHOD

1) Scrub oysters under running water.

2) Place them in a glass casserole dish.

3) Put them in microwave for 5 minutes on warm.

4) Remove from oven, pry open and shuck at once. Using this method, the oysters will be uncooked.

You can completely open oysters by putting them in the microwave for 3 minutes on high. The oysters will be thoroughly cooked.

If you don't happen to own a microwave, you may want to try the oven-and-ice-water technique. Preheat oven to 400°F and scrub oysters. Place oysters on a cookie sheet in middle of oven for 5 minutes. Have ready a dishpan or a sinkful of ice water. Immediately dump oysters into the chilled water. The hinges will pry open easily.

*Raw oysters*

## OYSTERS ON THE HALF SHELL

For many true oyster lovers, raw on the half shell is the *only* way to savor their favorite shellfish. Most purists, however, will allow a squeeze of lemon or perhaps a spoonful of the classic sauce mignonnette. And in Louisiana a bottle of Tabasco pepper sauce is *de rigueur*. On the oyster bar at Pacific Heights Bar & Grill, we set out lemon wedges, Tabasco, horseradish, salt and pepper, our house-made fresh tomato salsa, sauce mignonnette and, of course, big glass goblets of oyster crackers.

To prepare oysters on the half shell, select uniformly shaped small to medium-size fresh oysters of your choice. Shuck just before serving, according to directions on preceding pages. For each serving, arrange 6 oysters on a bed of crushed ice on individual plates garnished with lemon wedges. You may serve them with any of the following sauces and toppings. Either spoon a bit of sauce on each oyster or serve bowls of several sauces so that guests may add their own toppings. Don't forget the oyster crackers.

## HOW TO EAT AN OYSTER

Most restaurants provide tiny forks with an order of raw oysters on the half shell. This is a mistake. There is only one way to properly enjoy a raw oyster. Pick the oyster shell up with your fingers, taking care not to spill the oyster liquor. Bring the broad end of the oyster to your lips, tip the shell and drink the juices, tilt your head back just slightly and if necessary nudge the oyster in with your fingertip.

*"Why should anyone need a recipe? Oysters are best fresh, cold, raw and plain."*

PHYLLIS C. RICHMAN

## MIGNONNETTE SAUCE

*Makes one cup*
1 shallot, peeled and minced
1 cup red wine vinegar
1 teaspoon freshly cracked
    black pepper
1 tablespoon fresh lemon juice

Combine all ingredients and
refrigerate until ready to serve
oysters.

## RED AND GREEN CHILI TOPPING FOR OYSTERS

This zippy topping is best with
full-flavored oysters, such as
Tomales Bay, Quilcene or
Chincoteague. Serve with ice-
cold vodka or your favorite
beer.

*Makes approximately one cup*
½-inch piece of fresh ginger,
    peeled and minced
1 shallot, minced
3 hot green chilies, seeded and
    minced
3 hot red chilies, seeded and
    minced
½ cup fresh lime juice
1 tablespoon cider vinegar
6 sprigs cilantro, minced
Pinch sugar

Mix all ingredients and chill.

## SPICY REMOULADE

*Makes one and one-half cups*
4 green onions, finely chopped
1 small rib celery, finely
    chopped
¼ cup hot mustard
½ cup mayonnaise
1½ tablespoons prepared
    horseradish
2 tablespoons olive oil
2 tablespoons finely chopped
    pimento
¼ cup tarragon vinegar
¼ cup chopped parsley
Cayenne pepper to taste
Salt to taste

Combine all ingredients, mixing well. Refrigerate until
ready to use.

## SHERRIED VINAIGRETTE

*Makes one cup*
1 shallot, peeled and minced
¾ cup sherry vinegar
2 tablespoons dry sherry
1 tablespoon lemon juice
1 teaspoon freshly cracked
    black pepper

Combine all ingredients and
refrigerate until ready to serve
oysters.

## WHAT TO DRINK AND EAT WITH AN OYSTER?

The English recommend
combining equal mea-
sures of champagne and
stout. Daniel Webster
washed down his oysters
with brandy and water.
But for most oyster lov-
ers, wine is the drink of
choice. "Chardonnay,
the grape of Chablis, is
traditionally the flavor
mate of oysters," says
Leon D. Adams, author
of *The Wines of America*,
"but Sauvignon Blanc
(Fume Blanc) and
Chenin Blanc harmonize
equally well."
As for complementary
foods, M. F. K. Fisher
likes "good crisp sour-
dough French bread,
with sweet butter—or
the conventional dark
bread, thinly sliced and
buttered." And for Phyl-
lis Richman the choice is
easy: "More oysters."

## FRESH TOMATO SALSA

This lively fresh topping will keep for three or four days, tightly covered in the refrigerator. Make a big batch of it to use with other dishes.

*Makes four cups*
5 ripe medium-size tomatoes, finely diced
5 green onions (white and green part), chopped
5 jalapeño peppers, seeded and finely chopped
1 cup cilantro, chopped
1 tablespoon chopped fresh oregano
Juice of 3 limes
Juice of 2 lemons
1 tablespoon red wine vinegar
¼ cup olive oil
1 teaspoon ground cumin
Salt and pepper to taste

Blend all ingredients well. Cover and refrigerate several hours to blend flavors.

*Oysters on the half shell, with various toppings: (clockwise from bottom) Red and Green Chili, Fresh Tomato Salsa and Fresh Cucumber Relish.*

## FRESH CUCUMBER RELISH

*Makes one and one-half cups*
1 medium-size cucumber, peeled, seeded and finely diced
1 ripe tomato, peeled, seeded and finely diced
1 tablespoon snipped fresh dill
1 tablespoon fresh lemon juice
1 tablespoon cider vinegar
1 teaspoon dry sherry
Cracked black pepper to taste
Pinch cayenne pepper
Salt to taste
Lemon wedges and fresh dill sprigs for garnish

Combine all ingredients. Refrigerate until ready to use.

## OYSTER SHOOTER

Some people like to drink their raw oysters. The oyster shooter is a popular drink at Pacific Heights Bar & Grill.

In a shot glass put one shucked raw oyster, add 1 ounce vodka, a pinch horseradish, a dab cocktail sauce and a dash Tabasco pepper sauce.

## OYSTER CEVICHE

*Serves eight*
40 large fresh oysters
1¼ cups fresh lime juice
½ small yellow onion, minced
½ small red onion, minced
3 green onions, minced
5 cloves garlic, minced
2 tablespoons chopped fresh coriander
¾ teaspoon Dijon-style mustard
1 teaspoon white wine vinegar
½ teaspoon salt
1 fresh jalapeño pepper, seeded and finely chopped
1 teaspoon Thai chili paste* or ½ teaspoon Tabasco pepper sauce
1 teaspoon sugar
1 ripe tomato, peeled, seeded and diced

*Available in Oriental and specialty food shops.

Shuck oysters, drain and set aside. Mix well all other ingredients and gently fold in oysters. Refrigerate for at least 1 hour. To serve, spoon oyster mixture back into half shell or arrange on a bed of crisp lettuce with sliced avocado.

SUGGESTED OYSTERS   Large, firm: Bluepoint or Yaquina Bay.

*Hot on the half shell*

## BAKED OYSTERS WITH PARMESAN

*Serves four*
1 tablespoon fine dry bread
   crumbs
¼ pound butter, melted
1 teaspoon lemon juice
1 teaspoon Pernod
1 tablespoon minced green
   onions
1 tablespoon minced red bell
   pepper
Pinch cayenne pepper
Pinch salt
1 tablespoon chopped parsley
16 fresh oysters on the half
   shell
Rock salt, to cover a small baking pan ¼ inch deep
Grated parmesan cheese

Preheat oven to 425°F. In a
small bowl, combine bread
crumbs, melted butter, lemon
juice, Pernod, green onions,
red pepper, cayenne, salt and
parsley. Stir to combine well.
Arrange oysters on rock salt
and sprinkle 1 teaspoon of
mixture onto each oyster.
Then sprinkle each oyster with
parmesan. Bake 10 to 12 minutes and serve hot.

SUGGESTED OYSTERS
Bluepoint, Chesapeake or
Chincoteague.

## OYSTERS KIRKPATRICK

Oysters Kirkpatrick was created by chef Ernest Arbogast
of the Palace Hotel in San
Francisco during the bawdy
Barbary Coast days, when the
Palace was an elegant retreat
for the city's upper crust. This
dish was named to honor the
hotel's manager Colonel John
C. Kirkpatrick.

*Serves four*
16 fresh oysters on the half
   shell
Rock salt, to cover a shallow
   baking pan ¼ inch deep
8 strips bacon, fried crisp,
   drained and crumbled
Sweet butter
Tomato catsup
Grated parmesan cheese

Preheat oven to 450° F.
Arrange oysters on rock salt.
Sprinkle with crumbled bacon
and top each with 1 teaspoon
butter and 1 teaspoon catsup;
then sprinkle generously with
parmesan. Bake until hot and
bubbly, about 10 minutes.

SUGGESTED OYSTERS   Strong
ocean-flavored oysters with a
fairly deep shell: Golden Mantle or Tomales Bay.

## BARBECUED OYSTERS PACIFIC HEIGHTS STYLE

We developed this recipe for the weekly oyster festivals at PHB&G. It has become one of our most popular dishes.

*Serves four*

BARBECUE SAUCE
1 teaspoon minced fresh
    ginger
2 cloves garlic, minced
1 teaspoon Thai chili paste*
1 teaspoon sesame oil
2 tablespoons soy sauce
1½ cups light fish stock (page
    90) or chicken broth
¼ cup fresh lime juice
Salt to taste

16 fresh oysters on the half
    shell
Rock salt or bed of julienne-
    cut cabbage leaves for serv-
    ing plates
2 green onions, finely minced

*Available in Oriental and spe-
    cialty food shops.

Combine ingredients for sauce, which may be made ahead of time. Place oysters directly on hot barbecue grill, about 3 inches from hot coals. Top each with 1 tablespoon of barbecue sauce and grill until hot and bubbly. Transfer to serving plates and sprinkle with green onions. Serve hot.

SUGGESTED OYSTERS    Large, deep-cupped varieties: Tomales Bay, Bluepoint, Portuguese.

## BROILED OYSTERS WITH BACON AND SHALLOTS

*Serves four*
½ cup diced bacon
5 tablespoons sweet butter
2 shallots, finely chopped
½ cup fine dry bread crumbs
¼ cup lemon juice
½ teaspoon Pernod
¼ cup chopped parsley
¼ cup grated romano cheese
24 fresh oysters on the half
    shell
Rock salt to cover a shallow
    baking pan ¼ inch deep

In a small skillet, sauté bacon until crisp; remove bacon from skillet, drain and crumble. Wipe the skillet clean and melt butter in it. Sauté shallots until golden brown, about 4 minutes. Add bread crumbs and sauté until butter is absorbed. Remove skillet from heat, add lemon juice, Pernod, parsley, bacon and cheese. Stir to combine.

Preheat broiler. Arrange oysters on rock salt in baking pan and top each with 1 tablespoon of the sauté mixture. Broil 4 inches from heat source until bubbly and lightly browned, about 3 to 4 minutes. Serve hot.

SUGGESTED OYSTERS
Plump, mild, ocean flavored: Willapa Bay or Kumamoto.

*In seventeenth-century England, a fire-eater named Richardson would place a live coal on his tongue and a raw oyster on the coal. The coal was fanned with bellows until the oyster was broiled.*

# OYSTERS ROCKEFELLER

This classic oyster dish, with its sumptuous ingredients, is said to be as rich as Rockefeller. Created in 1899 by Jules Alciatore, the chef of New Orleans' renowned Antoine's restaurant. The original recipe is a well-kept secret, but a New York chef, Louis P. De Gouy, claims to have written down the instructions from Alciatore. The ingredients include green onions, celery, chervil, tarragon, bread crumbs, Tabasco, butter and absinthe. There is no mention of spinach, which many consider a basic component in its preparation.

There are possibly as many variations on this dish as there are oysters in the sea; for your dining pleasure we offer you one more.

*Serves four*
3 green onions (white part and 1 inch of green), minced
1 rib celery, finely diced
4 tablespoons butter
1 cup chopped fresh spinach (1 small bunch)
2 tablespoons fine dry bread crumbs
Dash Tabasco pepper sauce
¼ teaspoon Worcestershire sauce
¼ pound butter, softened
2 strips bacon, fried crisp, then crumbled
Salt to taste
24 fresh oysters on the half shell
Rock salt or crumpled foil

Preheat oven to 450°F. Sauté onions and celery in butter until tender. Add chopped spinach and cook 1 minute; remove from heat. Add bread crumbs, Tabasco, Worcestershire and salt. Blend together with the softened butter and bacon.

In a shallow baking pan large enough to hold all the oysters, put enough rock salt (or foil) to keep the oysters from tipping over. Arrange oysters in pan and top each with about 1 teaspoon of the sauté mixture. Bake 10 minutes until hot and bubbly. Serve at once.

SUGGESTED OYSTERS    Chincoteague or James River.

## REMEMBER YOUR FIRST TIME?

We asked a sampling of distinguished wine and food experts to tell us about the first time they ate an oyster. "It was when I was about sixteen," M. F. K. Fisher recalls. "At the Christmas banquet in boarding school. I thought they were pretty horrible, because I had been brought up to believe that oysters were to be swallowed in one gulp by well-bred people, especially females."

Elaine Tait ate her first oysters when she was twelve. "My father brought back some oysters from a men's club clambake. I liked them, but probably because I wasn't expected to. When I told my mother I liked oysters, she made some comment about that being unfeminine."

# OYSTERS CASINO

*Serves four*
4 slices bacon, chopped
1 rib celery, chopped
1 small onion, chopped
4 tablespoons butter
1 teaspoon lemon juice
1 teaspoon salt
Pinch black pepper
1 teaspoon Worcestershire
  sauce
A few drops Tabasco pepper
  sauce
¼ cup chopped fresh parsley
Rock salt
24 fresh oysters on the half
  shell

Preheat oven to 400° F. Fry bacon until partially crisp. Add celery, onion and butter; cook until tender. Add lemon juice, salt, pepper, Worcestershire, Tabasco and parsley. Stir to combine.

Arrange oysters in a roasting pan on rock salt or on individual heat-proof serving plates. Spread bacon mixture over oysters. Bake in hot oven until hot and bubbly or place under broiler for about 5 minutes.

SUGGESTED OYSTERS  Chesapeake or Bluepoint.

*Chef Louis de Gouy claimed that you can intoxicate an oyster by immersing him in carbonated water for five minutes. The oyster will relax its muscles and will be easier to shuck.*

# SPARKLING OYSTERS BEURRE ROSE

*Serves four*
1½ cups rosé champagne
4 tablespoons red wine vinegar
2 shallots, minced
¼ pound butter, softened
1 clove garlic, minced
1 tablespoon lemon juice
2 tablespoons minced chives
1 tablespoon minced parsley
Salt to taste
16 fresh oysters on the half
  shell
½ cup fine dry bread crumbs
Rock salt, to cover a small baking pan ¼ inch deep

Preheat broiler. In a small saucepan, combine champagne, vinegar and shallots. Cook over high heat until almost dry (to the consistency of marmalade). Remove from heat and cool somewhat, then blend in a food processor, or a mixing bowl, with butter, garlic, lemon juice, chives, parsley and salt.

Arrange oysters on rock salt. Spoon about 1 teaspoon of butter mixture on top of each oyster. Sprinkle lightly with bread crumbs. Broil 3 to 4 minutes, 3 inches from heat source, until hot and bubbly. Serve immediately.

SUGGESTED OYSTERS  Belon or Black Bay.

*"Oysters are not really food, but are relished to bully the sated stomach into further eating."*

SENECA

*Appetizers*

## MARINATED OYSTERS WITH GARLIC AND SHERRY VINEGAR

*Serves four*
½ cup olive oil
24 fresh oysters, shucked and
  drained
4 cloves garlic, thinly sliced
½ cup dry white wine
3 tablespoons sherry vinegar
2 bay leaves
6 whole peppercorns
¼ teaspoon dried tarragon
Salt to taste

Heat a medium-size skillet
until hot. Lightly oil the bottom of it with 1 teaspoon of the
olive oil. Add oysters and toss
in pan for just 15 seconds;
remove and cool. In the same
pan heat remaining olive oil.
Sauté garlic until golden;
remove from heat. Add wine,
vinegar, bay leaves, peppercorns, tarragon and salt. Cool
completely and pour over oysters. Cover and marinate 6
hours or overnight. Serve on
crackers or plain toast points.

SUGGESTED OYSTERS   Hog
Island Sweetwater, Belon or
New Zealand Kiwi.

## OYSTERS IN SAFFRON SAUCE

*Serves six*
2 tablespoons olive oil
1 medium-size onion, chopped
2 cloves garlic, minced
2 medium-size ripe tomatoes,
  peeled, seeded and diced
1 bay leaf
Pinch red pepper flakes
¼ cup brandy
1½ cups chicken stock
24 fresh oysters, shucked,
  liquor reserved
Salt and pepper to taste
Chopped parsley

Heat oil in a deep, heavy-
bottomed skillet. Sauté onion
and garlic until onion is soft.
Stir in tomatoes, bay leaf and
pepper flakes. Cook over
medium heat 3 to 4 minutes
until tomatoes begin to break
down. Add brandy and cook 1
minute. Add stock and simmer
until sauce is slightly thickened. Stir in oysters and oyster
liquor, salt and pepper to taste.
Cook just until oysters plump
and edges curl. Spoon hot onto
serving plates. Sprinkle with
chopped parsley. This dish is
good served over a small
amount of cooked rice.

SUGGESTED OYSTERS   Large
Bluepoint or Portuguese.

## WARM SPINACH SALAD WITH OYSTERS, PANCETTA AND PEPPERS

This salad was created for Pacific Heights Bar and Grill's New Year's Eve menu. It is a celebration of the best that California has to offer—crisp spinach, fresh red peppers and plump Tomales Bay oysters. Any day can be a holiday when you serve this salad.

*Serves four*
3 ounces pancetta (cured Italian bacon), thinly sliced and diced
1 medium-size red bell pepper, cut in thin julienne
2 tablespoons champagne vinegar
3 tablespoons mild olive oil
Salt and pepper to taste
20 fresh oysters, shucked, liquor reserved
1 bunch fresh spinach leaves, washed and dried

Sauté pancetta in a skillet until crisp. Add peppers and cook until slightly softened, about 1 minute. Add vinegar and cook 1 minute. Add oil, salt and pepper, oysters and oyster

*Warm Spinach Salad*

liquor. Cook just until oysters are warmed. Remove from heat. Arrange spinach leaves on 4 plates. Spoon oysters onto spinach and drizzle the warm dressing over them.

SUGGESTED OYSTERS
Medium size, creamy: James River, Malpeque or Tomales Bay.

## WARM OYSTER AND SCALLOP RAGOUT

*Serves four*
2 tablespoons olive oil
½ pound sea scallops, cleaned
16 oysters, shucked, liquor reserved
1 tablespoon shallots, finely chopped
¼ cup dry white wine
1 teaspoon lemon juice
1 tablespoon white wine vinegar
¼ teaspoon ground saffron threads
1 small red bell pepper, cut in 1-inch julienne
¼ pound plus 4 tablespoons sweet butter, cut in small pieces
Pinch cayenne pepper
2 tablespoons snipped fresh chives
2 tablespoons heavy cream
Salt and cracked black pepper to taste

Heat oil in a medium-size sauté pan. Add scallops and cook, browning quickly on each side, approximately 2 minutes. Remove scallops from pan with a slotted spoon and keep warm. Pour off oil. Add oysters to hot pan and immediately turn them once; after 30 seconds remove oysters and keep them warm with scallops. In the same pan add shallots, wine, lemon juice, vinegar, saffron and bell pepper. Reduce over high heat, until only 1 tablespoon liquid remains. On lowest possible heat whisk in butter, 1 tablespoon at a time, until fully incorporated. Add cayenne, chives, cream, salt and pepper. Add scallops and oysters to warm sauce and serve immediately.

SUGGESTED OYSTERS
Yaquina Bay or Willapa Bay.

*"He was a bold man
who first ate
an oyster."*

JONATHAN SWIFT

63

## OYSTERS IN HERBED CUSTARD

*Serves four*
¼ pound sweet butter
3 tablespoons flour
1 teaspoon salt
¼ teaspoon white pepper
1 tablespoon chopped summer
    savory
2 tablespoons chopped chives
1 tablespoon fresh lemon juice
Reserved oyster liquor and
    chicken stock to make 1½
    cups liquid
¼ cup dry sherry
3 egg yolks, beaten lightly
24 oysters shucked, liquor
    reserved
Fine dry bread crumbs

Preheat broiler. In a double boiler melt butter. Blend in flour, salt and pepper; cook 3 to 4 minutes. Add savory, chives, lemon juice, stock, sherry and egg yolks; cook, stirring until thickened.

Divide oysters among 4 individual flame-proof dishes. Top with custard and sprinkle with bread crumbs. Place under broiler, 3 inches from heat source, until bread crumbs are nicely browned. Serve at once.

SUGGESTED OYSTERS    Mild, meaty textured: Alabama Gulf or Kumamoto.

*"Oyster cellars—
pleasant retreats
say I."*

CHARLES DICKENS

## OYSTER AND CORN FRITTERS

*Makes twelve 4-inch fritters*
1 cup milk
½ cup heavy cream
1 egg
1 egg yolk
2 tablespoons flat beer
1 cup plus 2 tablespoons all-
    purpose flour
1 teaspoon baking powder
1 teaspoon salt
¼ teaspoon pepper
Pinch cayenne pepper
1 small red bell pepper,
    seeded and finely chopped
1 cup fresh corn kernels (2 to 3
    ears)
20 fresh oysters, shucked,
    drained and chopped
Sweet butter for cooking
Sour cream and chopped
    chives or Spicy Remoulade
    (page 53) for garnish

In a medium-size mixing bowl, whisk together milk, cream, egg, egg yolk and beer. Sift together flour, baking powder, salt, pepper and cayenne; mix well into wet ingredients. Stir in bell pepper and corn. Refrigerate until ready to use.

On a griddle or large skillet melt 1 tablespoon butter. For each fritter, pour about ½ cup batter onto cooking surface and scatter 1 tablespoon chopped oysters on top. Cook until bubbles form, 2 to 3 minutes. Turn and cook 2 to 3 more minutes, until golden brown. Serve with sour cream and chopped chives or Spicy Remoulade.

SUGGESTED OYSTERS
Golden Mantle or Portuguese.

## SCALLOPED OYSTERS

In 1913, on the lower level of New York City's then newly renovated railroad station, The Grand Central Oyster Bar & Restaurant opened for business. Today as then, they serve a dish called scalloped oysters. In honor of The Grand Central Oyster Bar, we've cooked up our own scalloped oysters.

*Serves four*
3 tablespoons sweet butter
2 tablespoons chopped shallots
½ cup finely diced celery
1½ cups cracker crumbs
1 cup heavy cream
Salt and black pepper
Pinch cayenne pepper
24 fresh oysters, shucked and
    drained

Preheat oven to 375° F. Butter
a 1-quart shallow gratin dish.
In a small skillet, melt butter
and sauté shallots and celery 3
to 4 minutes. Remove from
heat and stir in cracker
crumbs. In a small bowl, mix
cream, salt, pepper and cayenne to taste. Spread half the
crumb mixture in gratin dish.
Arrange oysters over crumbs.
Pour cream mixture over oysters and top with remaining
crumb mixture. Bake 20 minutes or until crumbs are
browned.

SUGGESTED OYSTERS  Blue-
point or Chincoteague.

## ANGELS ON HORSEBACK

While many people believe
that Angels on Horseback is
classic New England fare, the
recipe actually dates back to

Victorian England, when oysters were so plentiful they
were eaten mainly by the poor.

*Serves four*
16 fresh oysters, shucked,
    liquor reserved
8 slices bacon, cut in half
Melted butter
16 toothpicks
16 thinly sliced buttery toast
    points
Lemon wedges

Preheat broiler. Heat a small
sauté pan until hot. Add oysters and their liquor to pan and
quickly toss to lightly poach
them, about 30 seconds.
Remove oysters from pan and
wrap each one in bacon, secur-
ing with a toothpick. Sprinkle
with melted butter and broil, 3
inches from heat source, turn-
ing 3 to 4 times until bacon is
cooked. Remove toothpicks
and serve oysters on the buttery toast points with lemon
wedges.

SUGGESTED OYSTERS  Small
to medium size, plump and
creamy: Willapa Bay, Kumamoto, Hog Island Sweetwater
or Gulf.

## PEPPERED OYSTERS WITH COGNAC AND CREAM

*Serves four*
16 oysters, shucked, liquor
    reserved
Freshly cracked black pepper
3 tablespoons butter
1 tablespoon chopped shallots
2 tablespoons cognac
1 teaspoon lemon juice
1 cup heavy cream
Salt to taste
Sour cream for garnish

Lightly sprinkle oysters with
cracked black pepper. Melt
butter in a heavy-bottomed
skillet, add oysters and sauté
until edges just begin to curl.
Remove oysters with a slotted
spoon and set aside. Pour off
all but 1 tablespoon of the butter. Add shallots to pan and
sauté briefly. Add cognac,
lemon juice and reserved oyster liquor; reduce over high
heat to 2 tablespoons. Add
cream and salt to taste; cook to
thicken sauce somewhat.
Return oysters to pan and heat
through. Spoon onto warm
serving dishes and top with a
small dollop of sour cream.

SUGGESTED OYSTERS  Large,
firm types: Bluepoint, Malpeque or Yaquina Bay.

*Soups*

## CORN AND OYSTER CHOWDER

*Serves six*

4 strips bacon
1 small onion, chopped
1 cup diced celery
1 large potato, peeled and
  diced
1 carrot, peeled and diced
24 medium-size oysters,
  shucked, liquor reserved
1½ cups light fish stock (page
  90)
1½ cups fresh corn kernels
  (frozen if fresh not available)
1½ cups fresh green peas (or
  frozen)
2 cups milk
½ cup chopped fresh parsley
1 tablespoon chopped fresh
  oregano
1½ teaspoons salt
¼ teaspoon white pepper
Dash Tabasco pepper sauce
¼ cup cornstarch

Cook bacon in large saucepan over moderate heat until half cooked. Remove bacon from pan and crumble when cool. Sauté onion in bacon fat until slightly tender. Add celery, potato, carrot, oyster liquor and fish stock. Simmer until carrots and potatoes are tender. Add corn, peas, 1 cup of the milk, parsley, oregano, salt, pepper and Tabasco. In a small bowl combine remaining cup of milk with cornstarch and mix until smooth. Pour cornstarch mixture into large saucepan with other ingredients and whisk to combine. Continue to simmer partially covered for 12 to 15 minutes. Add oysters and simmer 3 minutes more.

SUGGESTED OYSTERS   Rhode Island Select, Chesapeake, or Bluepoint.

> *"If they must be cooked,*
> *which is basically*
> *a pity, an oyster stew*
> *is probably the best."*

M. F. K. FISHER

## NEW ENGLAND–STYLE OYSTER STEW

After an arduous journey on the *Mayflower*, Edward Winslow sent letters back to England about the bountiful food in the New World. Indians supplied the settlers with oysters, since the Pilgrims had none close at hand. The Indians preferred to eat their oysters cooked and perhaps they shared their recipe for oyster stew with the colonists.

By the nineteenth century, Sunday evenings were oyster-stew nights. In New England kitchens, the head of the house would work his culinary wizardry and produce a piping hot oyster stew for the family to devour. You don't have to wait for Sunday to make our recipe for oyster stew.

*Serves four*
20 fresh oysters, shucked, liquor reserved
1 tablespoon fresh thyme
½ teaspoon celery salt
Pinch cayenne pepper
2 cups heavy cream
2 cups milk
4 tablespoons sweet butter, cut in small pieces
Salt and pepper to taste
¼ cup chopped fresh parsley

In a large saucepan, heat oyster liquor with thyme, celery salt and cayenne. Add oysters and cook until their edges just begin to curl. Add cream, milk and butter. Heat slowly, stirring gently; do not boil. Season with salt and pepper. Add chopped parsley and serve in warm soup bowls.

SUGGESTED OYSTERS   Chesapeake Bay or Rhode Island Select.

## THAI-STYLE OYSTER BROTH WITH SALMON AND CILANTRO

*Serves four*
1 large clove garlic, minced
2 shallots, minced
2 leeks (white part and ½-inch of green), cut in 1-inch julienne
1 cup clam juice
3 cups water
1 teaspoon fish sauce*
1 teaspoon Thai chili paste*
12 large fresh oysters, shucked, liquor reserved
1 large zucchini, cut in 1-inch julienne
1 tomato, peeled, seeded and cut in julienne
1 8-ounce salmon fillet, cut into 8 1-ounce squares
Salt and pepper to taste
4 tablespoons butter, softened
1 cup loosely packed cilantro leaves

*Available at Oriental and specialty food shops.

Place garlic, shallots, leeks, clam juice and water in a large saucepan and bring to a boil. Reduce heat and simmer 15 to 20 minutes. Blend fish sauce and chili paste; add to broth. Add reserved oyster liquor, zucchini, tomato, salmon and oysters. Cook until salmon turns opaque and oysters curl. Salt and pepper to taste. Place 1 tablespoon butter and ¼ cup cilantro in each of 4 bowls and ladle hot broth into bowls. Serve at once.

SUGGESTED OYSTERS Willapa Bay or Quilcene.

## SOUTHERN-STYLE PEANUT BUTTER AND OYSTER SOUP

Long before the United States was colonized, black cooks in their native Africa were cooking with peanuts. In the Old South the plantation kitchen slaves created an imaginative soup made of peanut butter and oyster liquor. This rather odd-sounding combination makes a wonderfully rich soup, perfect to serve on a cool winter night in Virginia.

*Serves four*
3 tablespoons sweet butter
5 green onions, minced
½ cup smooth peanut butter
2 tablespoons flour
2 cups chicken stock (if using canned broth, use 1 8-ounce can plus 1 can water)
½ cup heavy cream
1 teaspoon chopped fresh savory

⅛ teaspoon cayenne pepper
Salt to taste
3 tablespoons dry sherry
24 oysters, shucked, liquor reserved
¼ cup chopped parsley

In a heavy-bottomed 2-quart saucepan, melt butter and sauté green onions on medium heat for 2 minutes. Blend in peanut butter, then flour. Cook, stirring constantly, for 3 minutes. Turn heat to very low and gradually whisk in stock and reserved oyster liquor. Increase heat and simmer for 12 to 15 minutes; stir often. Add cream, savory, cayenne and salt to taste. Stir in sherry, then add oysters. Cook 1 to 2 minutes to heat oysters. Serve in warm soup bowls and sprinkle with chopped parsley.

SUGGESTED OYSTERS Creamy, small to medium size: Alabama Gulf or Emerald Point.

*"Eat oysters,
love longer."*

OYSTER INSTITUTE
OF AMERICA

## OYSTER AND SPINACH SOUP

*Serves four*
2 tablespoons sweet butter
1 medium-size leek (white part and 1 inch of green), diced
1 cup washed, finely chopped spinach
1 teaspoon Pernod
16 fresh oysters, shucked, liquor reserved
2 cups heavy cream
2 cups milk
1 cup chicken stock
¼ teaspoon dry mustard
Pinch cayenne pepper
Salt to taste

In a large saucepan, melt butter over moderate heat. Add diced leek and cook until tender, about 3 to 4 minutes, being careful not to brown. Add spinach and cook, stirring, until wilted, about 3 minutes. Add Pernod, oyster liquor, cream, milk, stock, dry mustard, cayenne and salt. Bring to a boil, then lower heat to simmer 5 minutes. Stir in oysters and cook just until their edges begin to curl, about 1 minute. Serve in warm, shallow soup bowls.

SUGGESTED OYSTERS Bluepoint or Chesapeake.

*Light entrees*

## OYSTERS BENEDICT

*Serves four*
2 cups Dilled Hollandaise
  Sauce, following
Butter
4 English muffins, split in half
8 eggs
1 teaspoon white vinegar
8 large fresh oysters, shucked
  and drained

Preheat broiler. Prepare Dilled
Hollandaise and keep warm.
Butter muffin halves and toast
in broiler. Poach eggs in a simmering pan of water with vinegar for about 4 minutes, until
set. Add oysters to pan and
while they are poaching
remove eggs with a slotted
spoon, placing one on each
muffin half. When the edges
curl (1 minute), remove oysters with a slotted spoon and
place one next to each egg on
each muffin. Top with warm
Dilled Hollandaise.

SUGGESTED OYSTERS  Large
Bluepoint or Chesapeake.

## DILLED HOLLANDAISE SAUCE

*Makes two cups*
6 egg yolks
2 tablespoons lemon juice
2 tablespoons chopped fresh
  dill
Pinch cayenne pepper
½ pound butter, melted
Salt to taste

Put egg yolks in the top of a
double boiler or in a metal
bowl over simmering water,
and beat with a wire whisk
until smooth. Add lemon
juice, dill and cayenne pepper.
Gradually whisk in butter in a
thin steady stream. Sauce
should thicken. Thin sauce
with a tablespoon of warm
water, if necessary. Taste for
seasonings. Serve immediately
or hold in a warm place. If the
sauce separates, slowly beat in
a tablespoon cream until
smooth.

# OYSTER CREPES

*Makes eight crêpes*

## CREPES

¾ cup all-purpose flour
Pinch salt
2 eggs, beaten lightly
⅔ cup milk
1 tablespoon melted butter
Butter for cooking

Mix flour and salt. Mix together eggs, milk and melted butter. Gradually mix wet ingredients into dry and blend well. Cover and let sit for 30 minutes. Heat a small skillet or crêpe pan until moderately hot. Brush pan with a small amount of butter. Add 2 tablespoons of batter to pan, then quickly tilt the pan around so that the batter spreads evenly in the thinnest possible layer. Cook a few minutes until the bottom is lightly browned and the edges lift easily from pan. Crêpe should slide easily in pan. Turn crêpe with a small spatula and cook briefly (30 seconds). Remove crêpe from pan to a clean dry platter and keep warm in a low oven.

## FILLING

5 tablespoons butter
¼ cup all-purpose flour
1½ cups milk
3 ounces cream cheese, softened
1 small red bell pepper, seeded and chopped
1 rib celery, chopped
Salt and pepper to taste
1 tablespoon chopped fresh sage
16 oysters, shucked and drained, liquor reserved

Melt 4 tablespoons of the butter in a small saucepan. Gradually stir in flour. Add milk and cream cheese. Cook over medium heat until smooth. Measure out ½ cup of this mixture and reserve for sauce. Meanwhile heat remaining tablespoon butter in a small skillet. Sauté bell pepper and celery 3 to 4 minutes, until tender. Season with salt, pepper and sage. Fold into cream cheese mixture. Fold in oysters and heat mixture until hot.

## SAUCE

½ cup reserved cream sauce from filling mixture
¼ cup chopped parsley
1 tablespoon snipped fresh chives
Reserved oyster liquor
¼ cup milk
Salt to taste

Heat cream sauce. Whisk in parsley, chives, oyster liquor and milk. Salt to taste. Heat until smooth and hot.

## ASSEMBLY

Fill warm crêpes with filling; roll up and place seam side down on serving plates or platter. Pour hot sauce over crêpes. Serve immediately.

SUGGESTED OYSTERS   Kumamoto, Hog Island Sweetwater, Chesapeake or James River.

*During the reign of Emperor Diocletian (284–305 A.D.), the Roman monetary unit was equal to the value of one oyster.*

## OYSTER PIE

In the southern United States, oyster pie is a traditional side dish to be served with holiday turkey or ham. Oysters were so popular in the Old South that the streets of Biloxi, Mississippi, were once paved with oyster shells.

*Serves eight as side dish*
4 slices bacon, diced
1 onion, chopped
1 carrot, shredded
1 cup fresh corn kernels (2 to 3 ears)
1 cup fresh green peas
6 tablespoons butter
6 tablespoons all-purpose flour
20 oysters, shucked, liquor reserved
Reserved oyster liquor and chicken broth to make 2 cups liquid
1 cup heavy cream
Salt and pepper to taste
Pastry Crust, following

Preheat oven to 425°F. Sauté bacon until fairly crisp. Pour off half the accumulated fat and sauté onion until tender. Add carrot, corn and peas; sauté stirring 2 to 3 minutes, then set aside. Melt butter in a saucepan, stir in flour and cook, stirring, for 3 minutes. Slowly add broth, cream, salt and pepper. Cook for 5 minutes until thickened and smooth. Add vegetable mixture to sauce. Cut oysters in half and gently stir into mixture. Pour into a 9-inch pie pan or shallow casserole. Top with pastry crust; crimp edges and cut vents to allow steam to escape. Bake 25 to 30 minutes, until crust is nicely browned.

SUGGESTED OYSTERS    Firm, slightly salty: Quilcene or Bluepoint.

## PASTRY CRUST

*Makes one 9-inch shell*
2 cups all-purpose flour
½ teaspoon salt
⅔ cup shortening
5 to 6 tablespoons cold water

Mix flour and salt. Cut in shortening with a pastry blender or two knives; combine until mixture resembles coarse crumbs. Sprinkle water over flour mixture, a tablespoon at a time, and mix with a fork. When pastry begins to hold together, knead gently into a ball. Roll out dough slightly larger than the pan, so that there is a 1-inch overhang to crimp.

## OYSTER LOAF

In the nineteenth century, the oyster loaf was popular from Beacon Hill to the Gold Rush country. The original recipe was sheer simplicity: a toasted hollowed-out loaf of bread filled with sautéed oysters. An instant hit, the oyster loaf became more than a popular late-night snack—it became a tradition.

In New Orleans the oyster loaf had a special significance: It was known as *la médiatrice*— the mediator. After spending a night carousing in the French Quarter, a wayward husband would offer his enraged wife an oyster loaf as a peace offering.

New Orleans did not have an exclusive on philandering spouses. Mrs. James Monroe claims to have gotten her recipe for "The Peacemaker" (oyster loaf) from Mrs. George Washington. San Francisco had a version of the oyster loaf called "the squarer," and in Connecticut it was called "boxed oysters." We offer our own version of the oyster loaf, one that requires no act of indiscretion on the part of the diner.

*Serves four*

4 5-inch-long baguettes
16 fresh oysters, shucked and
  drained
2 eggs, beaten lightly
1½ cups fine dry bread crumbs
4 tablespoons sweet butter
¾ cup tartar sauce (6 ounces)
1 cup shredded lettuce
1 small tomato, diced

Preheat broiler. Cut baguettes in half lengthwise. With a small spoon, hollow out some of the soft white center of both halves about halfway down, forming a trench from end to end. Toast baguettes lightly in the broiler. Dip oysters first in eggs, then in bread crumbs. In a heavy-bottomed skillet heat butter until sizzling. Fry oysters in butter until golden brown on both sides; remove and drain on paper towels. Spread tartar sauce in hollowed-out baguettes, about 2 tablespoons in each. Place 4 oysters on the bottom half of each baguette. Top with shredded lettuce, diced tomato and the top half of the baguette.

SUGGESTED OYSTERS
Quilcene, Willapa Bay or
Portuguese.

*"I do not have a favorite oyster. Any good oyster, fresh and crisp from cold waters, is pure bliss for me."*

M. F. K. FISHER

## CALIFORNIA OYSTER OMELET

In the nineteenth century, chef Ernest Arbogast of the Palace Hotel in San Francisco cooked up an Olympia oyster omelet that was the toast of the Ladies' Grill. Here's our own version of his California omelet.

*Serves two*

1 ripe California avocado
6 eggs, beaten well
2 tablespoons sweet butter
1 small shallot, minced
2 mushroom caps, thinly sliced
1 tablespoon all-purpose flour
½ cup heavy cream
12 fresh oysters, shucked,
  liquor reserved
Salt and pepper to taste
Additional butter
Paprika

Peel avocado, cut in half and remove pit. Dice one half and cut other half into 4 slices; reserve. In a small skillet, melt butter and sauté shallots until tender, about 2 minutes; add mushrooms and sauté 2 minutes more. Stir in flour, then gradually add cream and reserved oyster liquor; cook over medium heat until thickened. Add oysters and cook until they plump. Remove from heat; stir in diced avocado, salt and pepper to taste.

Melt additional butter in an omelet pan or small skillet. Add eggs and cook slowly until eggs are as firm as you like them. Pour oyster mixture on one half, then fold eggs over. Cut in half and serve on warm plates. Garnish with avocado slices and paprika.

SUGGESTED OYSTERS  A plump, firm Pacific oyster with full flavor: Portuguese or Quilcene.

## OYSTERS WITH PANCETTA, LEEKS, FETTUCCINE AND CREAM

*Serves four*

2 tablespoons olive oil
4 ounces pancetta, diced
2 leeks (white part and 1 inch of green), cut in julienne
½ teaspoon minced garlic
4 sprigs fresh thyme
2 teaspoons lemon juice
1 teaspoon grated lemon rind
¼ cup dry white wine
16 fresh oysters, shucked, liquor reserved
1 cup heavy cream
Salt and pepper to taste
2 tablespoons chopped parsley
½ pound fresh fettuccine

In a large sauté pan, heat olive oil. Sauté pancetta until fairly crisp, 2 to 3 minutes. Add leeks and sauté quickly for 1 minute. Add garlic, thyme, lemon juice, rind and wine; cook on medium-high heat 1 to 2 minutes. Add reserved oyster liquor and reduce by half. Add cream and reduce to a light sauce consistency. Add oysters and cook just until the edges begin to curl. Add salt and pepper to taste and chopped parsley.

Cook fettuccine in rapidly boiling salted water for 1 minute. Drain and toss with sauce. Divide evenly on 4 warm plates. Garnish with thyme sprigs.

SUGGESTED OYSTERS   Chesapeake, Chincoteague or small Bluepoint.

## OVERHEARD AT THE PACIFIC HEIGHTS BAR & GRILL

"Our family got our own oysters from a sheltered cove on Chesapeake Bay. I have scars on the bottoms of my feet from collecting oysters."

"We never packed a lunch to go fishing off the reefs in Louisiana. We'd gather up oysters with our hands and eat them for lunch."

And from Anthony Chavez, on his tenth birthday: "I like oysters, oysters like me."

# HANGTOWN FRY

Hangtown Fry is a savory California omelet with an unsavory past. The recipe, as legend will have it, was the creation of a man about to be strung-up during the Gold Rush era. He wanted his last meal to combine all his favorite foods. But there is a less grisly version of the story: a forty-niner, pockets bursting with gold nuggets, rode into Hangtown (now Placerville) and demanded the most expensive meal the town had to offer. In the hills of the Gold Country, eggs, oysters and bacon were hard to come by, and so was born a California classic—Hangtown Fry. This omelet is at its best served with toasted slices of sourdough bread.

*Ulysses S. Grant, who frequented the Gold Country, had a fondness for pickled oysters.*

*Serves four*

16 fresh oysters, shucked and drained (reserve liquor for another use)
½ cup all-purpose flour
2 eggs, beaten well with salt and pepper to taste
½ cup dry bread crumbs, mixed with ½ cup yellow cornmeal
6 eggs
½ cup heavy cream
¼ pound sweet butter
8 slices bacon, fried crisp
Stewed Tomatoes, following

Roll oysters in flour, coating well; shake off excess flour, dip into the 2 beaten eggs, then roll oysters in bread crumb–cornmeal mixture; set aside. In a bowl mix the 6 eggs and cream; set aside.

In a large skillet melt butter until hot and sizzling. Add oysters and brown quickly on both sides. Pour eggs into skillet with oysters; reduce heat and cook until eggs are set and slightly browned underneath. Fold omelet over carefully into a half-circle. Divide into 4 equal portions and top each with 2 strips of bacon. Serve topped with Stewed Tomatoes.

SUGGESTED OYSTERS   This dish was originally made with Olympias, the only native Pacific Coast oyster—small, creamy and slightly salty. Use a small to medium-size oyster: New Zealand Kiwi, Kumamoto or Hog Island Sweetwater.

## STEWED TOMATOES

2 tablespoons butter
2 medium-size ripe tomatoes, peeled, seeded and diced
1 teaspoon fresh thyme (or ½ tablespoon dried)
1 clove garlic, minced
Salt and pepper to taste

Melt butter in a heavy saucepan. Add thyme and garlic. Stew 3 to 4 minutes. Adjust seasoning with salt and pepper.

*Shellfish stews*

## PACIFIC HEIGHTS BAR & GRILL SHELLFISH STEW

Mark Twain once said: "The coldest winter I ever spent was one summer in San Francisco." The cool, foggy summer evenings inspired this warming shellfish stew that we dedicate to Mr. Twain.

*Serves four*

12 fresh black mussels
12 small fresh clams
4 tablespoons butter
1 onion, finely chopped
1 tablespoon Worcestershire
    sauce
3 tablespoons chili sauce
1½ teaspoons paprika
1½ teaspoons celery salt
1 cup light fish stock (page 90)
    or ½ cup clam juice and ½
    cup water
8 medium-size shrimp, peeled
    and deveined
2 cups heavy cream
8 sea scallops
12 fresh oysters, shucked,
    liquor reserved
2 teaspoons snipped fresh
    chives

Scrub mussel and clam shells, but do not open. In a large, heavy casserole or Dutch oven, melt butter. Add onion and sauté over moderate heat until it just begins to brown. Add Worcestershire, chili sauce, paprika, celery salt, mussels and clams. Continue to cook until shells just begin to open. Add stock, increase heat to high and cook 3 to 4 minutes. Add shrimp and cream; cook 1 minute. Add scallops and cook 2 minutes. Add oysters and their liquor; cook until oysters plump and their edges begin to curl, about 1 minute. Divide into warm bowls. Garnish with chives and serve with crusty sourdough bread.

SUGGESTED OYSTERS   Portuguese, Quilcene or Tomales Bay.

# SHRIMP AND OYSTER JAMBALAYA

Jambalaya. Just the mention of the name makes us long for the bayou country, Mardi Gras and the streets of the Vieux Carré. This New Orleans culinary classic has two basic ingredients: rice and ham (jambon). Usually tomatoes, shrimp and other shellfish are added.

The Gulf Coast provides the riches of its sea for this Creole dish. But Louisiana is rich in something else—tradition. Each August in the fishing villages near New Orleans, an annual rite is held at dawn: the blessing of the shrimp fleet. After the archbishop bestows his blessing, the day becomes a festival. We can almost smell the steaming pots of jambalaya cooking on an open fire.

*Serves six*
2 cups water
½ cup dry white wine
1 bay leaf
5 whole peppercorns
¼ teaspoon salt
½ lemon
1 pound medium-size fresh shrimp
24 fresh oysters, shucked, liquor reserved
2 tablespoons sweet butter
1½ pounds smoked pork sausage, sliced in ½-inch rings
1 medium-size onion, finely chopped
2 medium-size green bell peppers, seeded and cut into 1½-inch julienne
1½ cups short-grain white rice
½ pound smoked ham
1 28-ounce can Italian plum tomatoes, chopped
3 cloves garlic, minced
1 tablespoon fresh thyme (1 teaspoon dried)
¼ teaspoon cayenne pepper
½ teaspoon chili powder
Pinch ground allspice or ground cloves
Pinch ground saffron threads (optional)
Salt and pepper to taste
12 fresh mussels in shells, scrubbed
12 fresh clams in shells, scrubbed
½ pound crab meat
Lemon wedges and chopped parsley for garnish

Combine water, white wine, bay leaf, peppercorns, salt and lemon. Bring to a boil. Add shrimp and cook 1 minute. Remove shrimp with a slotted spoon. Cool, devein and chop. Strain liquid and reserve to be used as stock.

In a large heavy-bottomed casserole with lid, heat butter, add sausage and onion and sauté until browned. Add bell pepper and sauté until limp and slightly browned. Add rice and cook, stirring constantly, until rice is slightly browned, about 5 minutes. Add ham, tomatoes, garlic, thyme, cayenne, chili powder, allspice, saffron and salt and pepper; stir to combine. Stir in ½ cup of reserved shrimp stock and cook 4 to 5 minutes, stirring often to avoid sticking. Add another ½ cup of stock, lower heat and simmer, partially covered, until stock is absorbed. Repeat this process with each half cup of stock. When the last of the stock is added, arrange mussels and clams around the side of casserole and cover completely to steam them open, 4 to 5 minutes. Then place shrimp, oysters and crab meat in the center of casserole, heating until the oysters begin to curl. Serve immediately. Garnish with lemon wedges and chopped parsley.

SUGGESTED OYSTERS  Gulf oysters.

# OYSTERS AND CLAMS MARINARA

*Serves four*
2 tablespoons olive oil
1 small onion, chopped
1 small green bell pepper, seeded and chopped
1 rib celery, chopped
2 cloves garlic, minced
2 tablespoons pitted and diced black olives
6 vine-ripened tomatoes, peeled, seeded and chopped or 1 28-ounce can Italian plum tomatoes
½ cup dry white wine
Reserved oyster liquor and water mixed to make 1½ cups stock
2 tablespoons chopped fresh oregano (2 teaspoon dried)
2 tablespoons chopped fresh basil (2 teaspoons dried)
Salt and black pepper to taste
16 fresh oysters, shucked and drained, liquor reserved
12 fresh cherrystone clams, in shells, scrubbed
4 cups cooked rice

In a medium to large covered pot or Dutch oven, heat olive oil. Sauté onion, bell pepper, and celery until tender. Add garlic, olives and tomatoes. Cook slowly for 5 minutes. Add wine, oyster stock, oregano, basil, salt and pepper. Stir and cook over medium heat for 10 minutes. Add clams, cover pot and cook until clams open, 3 to 4 minutes. Uncover and add oysters; cook 2 minutes more. Serve over hot cooked rice.

SUGGESTED OYSTERS   Large Bluepoint or Portuguese.

# SOUTHERN OYSTER STEW WITH TASSO AND RED BEANS

*Serves six*
⅔ cup peanut oil
⅔ cup all-purpose flour
1 onion, finely chopped
1 green bell pepper, chopped
2 ribs celery, chopped
2 large ripe tomatoes, peeled, seeded and chopped
1 cup cooked red beans
2 bay leaves
1 teaspoon cracked black pepper
1 teaspoon salt
½ teaspoon cayenne pepper
3 cloves garlic, minced
6 cups light fish stock (page 90)
6 ounces Cajun tasso, cut into 1-inch julienne, or smoked ham
24 fresh oysters, shucked, liquor reserved
½ cup heavy cream

Heat oil in a heavy-bottomed soup pot or Dutch oven until it begins to smoke, 3 to 4 minutes. Gradually add flour, whisking until smooth. Reduce heat to medium and continue to cook, stirring constantly until roux is a dark reddish-brown color. Immediately stir in chopped vegetables and beans. Stir and cook 3 to 4 minutes. Add bay leaves, pepper, salt, cayenne and garlic. Gradually whisk in stock. Simmer stew for 15 minutes. Add tasso, oysters, oyster liquor and cream. Cook until oysters plump and edges curl. Taste and adjust seasonings. Serve hot.

SUGGESTED OYSTERS   Apalachicola, Portuguese or large Bluepoint.

The Housekeepers Timetable *(1890) notes that stewed oysters take three hours and thirty minutes to digest, while roasted oysters take a mere three hours and fifteen minutes.*

# CIOPPINO

According to San Francisco legend, the fishermen along the wharf kept a pot of water, flavored with bits of garlic, tomato and onion, simmering on a charcoal brazier. Any unsold fish would be tossed in the stew pot. The base of the dish was more often than not Dungeness crab, which at the turn of the century sold for a mere dollar per sack.

Another local story holds that the stew got its name from the practice of San Franciscans who made the rounds of the fishing boats moored in the bay. "Chip in, chip in," they cried as they asked the fishermen for fish for their stew. Since most of the fishermen were from southern Italy they added an "o" to the words and thus was born a San Francisco original—cioppino.

There is probably some truth in both tales, but we know one thing for certain: From its humble origins, cioppino has developed into a wonderful fish stew—a delicate balance of seafood, wine and tomatoes.

*Serves eight*

2 tablespoons olive oil
2 tablespoons butter
3 cups chopped onions
4 large cloves garlic, finely minced
2 green bell peppers, seeded and chopped
8 tomatoes, peeled, seeded and chopped or 1 28-ounce can Italian plum tomatoes
1 cup tomato puree or sauce
½ cup chopped fresh basil
¼ cup chopped fresh oregano
3 tablespoons chopped fresh marjoram
¼ teaspoon cayenne pepper
2 cups light fish stock (page 90)
2 cups dry white wine
Salt and freshly ground pepper to taste
24 small fresh clams, in shells, scrubbed
16 fresh black mussels, in shells, scrubbed
2 fresh Dungeness crabs, cracked
1 pound firm-fleshed white fish, cubed
1 pound medium-size raw shrimp, peeled and deveined
24 fresh oysters, shucked, liquor reserved

Heat oil and butter in a large, heavy pot. Add onions and garlic; stir often and cook until onions are light golden in color. Add peppers and cook until they begin to soften. Add tomatoes, tomato puree, herbs and cayenne. Bring to a boil. Add fish stock and simmer 1 hour. Add wine and simmer an additional 30 minutes. Season with salt and pepper.

About 15 minutes before serving, add crab and simmer 5 minutes. Add clams, cover and cook 2 minutes. Add mussels and cook until they begin to open. Then add fish cubes and shrimp. Cook 3 minutes more. Add oysters and their liquor and cook 1 minute more. Serve in warm soup bowls with garlic toast or crusty sourdough bread.

SUGGESTED OYSTERS   Large, full flavored: Portuguese, Tomales Bay or Quilcene.

*Entrees*

## BAKED OYSTER AND WILD MUSHROOM CASSEROLE

*Serves eight*

24 fresh oysters, shucked, drained, liquor reserved
¼ pound butter
1 medium-size onion, diced
1 green bell pepper, seeded and diced
1½ pounds assorted wild mushrooms, sliced (tree oyster, Italian field, shiitake, hedgehog, chanterelle)
3 tablespoons chopped chives
Salt and pepper to taste
¼ cup all-purpose flour
1½ cups heavy cream
Reserved oyster liquor and milk combined to make 1 cup liquid
½ cup grated parmesan cheese
⅓ cup dry white wine
Fine dry bread crumbs

Preheat oven to 450°F. In a medium-size skillet, melt 4 tablespoons of the butter. Add onion and bell pepper; sauté until tender. Add mushrooms and chives; cook slowly for 5 minutes. Add salt and pepper to taste and set aside.

In a saucepan melt remaining 4 tablespoons butter; on low heat whisk in flour and cook 1 minute. Then slowly whisk in cream and oyster liquor–milk mixture. Simmer, stirring often, for 5 minutes until smooth and thick. Add 2 tablespoons of the cheese and all the wine. Cook 2 minutes more. Fold in oysters and mushroom mixture. Pour into a lightly buttered medium-size casserole or deep 10-inch pie pan. Combine remaining cheese with enough bread crumbs to cover and sprinkle over the top of the casserole. Bake 8 to 10 minutes until bubbly and lightly browned.

SUGGESTED OYSTERS
Strong, full-flavored: Golden Mantle or Malpeque.

## TEXAS-STYLE FRIED OYSTERS

*Serves four*
¾ cup all-purpose flour
½ cup yellow cornmeal
2 teaspoons salt
¾ teaspoon white pepper
¼ teaspoon onion powder
¼ teaspoon garlic powder
Pinch cayenne pepper
2 eggs
1 tablespoon milk
Vegetable oil for frying
24 fresh oysters, shucked and
   drained
Spicy Remoulade (page 53),
   Fresh Tomato Salsa (page
   55) or seafood sauce of
   choice

Combine all dry ingredients and mix well. Lightly beat together eggs and milk. Dip drained oysters first in flour mixture, next in egg mixture, then into flour mixture again. Shake off excess flour.

In a deep fryer or a deep heavy-bottomed skillet, heat oil to 375°F. Fry oysters in 3 batches until golden brown, about 2 minutes. Remove, drain on paper towels and keep warm in a low oven until all oysters are fried. Serve with Spicy Remoulade, Fresh Tomato Salsa or your favorite sauce for seafood.

SUGGESTED OYSTERS
Medium to large Gulf
varieties.

## TEXAS GULF OYSTER ROAST

A barbecue in Texas isn't just a barbecue. It's an event. Get yourself a bushel of Gulf oysters and a case of Lone Star beer and have yourself a good ol' time. Authentic Texas barbecues use mesquite wood. Though mesquite is the fuel of choice for cookouts, Indians once used the bean pods from mesquite to make soup and beer.

On the beach or at home, for this meal have lots of oysters on hand. Large deep-shelled varieties are best. Prepare a hot fire of mesquite or your favorite charcoal and place the grilling surface three to four inches above the hot coals.

1 pound sweet butter
Juice of 3 lemons
2 teaspoons freshly cracked
   black pepper
1 teaspoon salt
10 to 12 oysters (unshucked
   and scrubbed) per person
Lemon wedges
Tabasco pepper sauce

In a small heat-proof container, combine butter, lemon juice, pepper and salt. Place at edge of grill to melt and keep warm. Place unshucked oysters directly on grill and cover with grill top or a loose tent of foil. Cook 5 to 6 minutes until oysters open. Arrange on serving dishes, and serve hot with warm lemon butter and lemon wedges. Pass Tabasco sauce for those who like a bit of fire.

SUGGESTED OYSTERS   Texas Gulf, of course.

## OYSTER-STUFFED BAKED TROUT WITH ORANGE-SHALLOT BUTTER

*Serves six*
1 small carrot, finely diced
1 bunch leeks (white part and ½ inch of green), trimmed and cut thinly crosswise
4 tablespoons butter
2 cups cooked brown rice
18 oysters, shucked, drained and chopped
1 large egg, beaten lightly
2 tablespoons fine dry bread crumbs
¼ cup minced parsley
2 teaspoons grated orange rind
Salt and pepper to taste
6 boneless whole trout, 12 ounces each
3 tablespoons melted butter
Juice of ½ lemon
Orange-Shallot Butter, following

In a heavy skillet cook carrot and leeks in butter over medium heat until tender, about 5 minutes. Remove from heat and stir in rice, oysters, egg, bread crumbs, parsley, orange rind, salt and pepper. Mix well and set aside.

Preheat oven to 400°F. Fill cavity of each trout with some of the stuffing and fold over. Arrange trout in a lightly buttered baking pan. Brush with melted butter and squeeze juice of ½ lemon over all. Bake for 20 to 25 minutes until skin is brown and crisp. Serve with Orange-Shallot Butter.

SUGGESTED OYSTERS    Olympia or Kumamoto.

*In Rector's* **Naughty 90s Cookbook,** *the recipe for Fillet of Sole Marguery à la Diamond Jim Brady is garnished with a dozen poached oysters.*

## ORANGE-SHALLOT BUTTER

¼ cup dry white wine
2 tablespoons white wine vinegar
2 tablespoons finely chopped shallots
Juice of 1 orange
¼ teaspoon salt
Pinch white pepper
½ pound butter, chilled and cut into small pieces

In a small, heavy-bottomed saucepan, combine wine, vinegar, shallots, orange juice, salt and pepper. Reduce over high heat to 1 to 2 tablespoons. Remove pan from heat and whisk in several tablespoons butter, about 1 tablespoon at a time. On lowest possible heat, whisk in remaining butter piece by piece. The butter must not melt, but form a creamy emulsion. When all butter is incorporated, turn off heat and keep sauce in a warm place until ready to use.

## SEA SCALLOPS AND OYSTERS BAKED IN PARCHMENT

*Serves four*

3 tablespoons olive oil
1 carrot cut in 1-inch julienne
1 leek (white part), cut in 1-inch julienne
½ pound mushrooms, thinly sliced
¼ cup coarsely chopped parsley
4 tablespoons fresh lime juice
4 tablespoons dry white wine
Salt, freshly ground black pepper
4 tablespoons sweet butter
½ pound sea scallops
16 fresh oysters, shucked and drained
4 pieces bakers' parchment or foil, approximately 12 × 14 inches

Preheat oven to 475°F. In a heavy skillet heat olive oil. Add carrots and sauté for 2 minutes. Add leeks and mushrooms and cook until they begin to soften. Remove from heat and stir in parsley. Let cool. Fold each piece of parchment or foil in half and cut into a lopsided oval, the shape of half a heart. Divide vegetable mixture evenly between the 4 hearts. Top each with one fourth of the scallops and 4 oysters. Sprinkle each package with 1 tablespoon lime juice, 1 tablespoon white wine, salt and pepper to taste; top with 1 tablespoon butter. Seal packages by folding, starting at one end and overlapping folds. Lightly brush tops and edges of parchment with olive oil and place on a baking sheet in hot oven for 10 to 12 minutes. Serve warm, slicing parchment open with a sharp knife and peeling back paper.

SUGGESTED OYSTERS   Apalachicola, Black Bay or other mild, small to medium-size Florida or Gulf oysters.

## OYSTER AND SMOKED-HAM STUFFING FOR TURKEY

*Stuffs a 10- to 12-pound turkey*

4 tablespoons butter
2 medium-size onions
1 green bell pepper, diced
3 ribs celery, thinly sliced
2 tablespoons chopped fresh sage (1 tablespoon dried)
½ pound smoked ham, cut in ¼-inch dice
1 cup chopped walnuts
1 cup fresh coarsely chopped parsley
2 cups dry ¼-inch bread cubes
3 eggs, beaten lightly
24 fresh oysters, shucked and diced, liquor reserved
Salt and pepper to taste

In a large skillet melt butter. Add onions, bell pepper and celery. Sauté until tender, 4 to 5 minutes. Add sage, ham and walnuts; cook, stirring, 3 minutes more. Remove from heat. Stir in parsley, bread cubes, eggs, oysters and liquor. Add salt and pepper to taste.

SUGGESTED OYSTERS   Full-flavored: Quilcene, Golden Mantle or Malpeque.

*Sea Scallops and Oysters Baked in Parchment*

## OYSTER-CORNBREAD STUFFING FOR TURKEY

*Stuffs a 10- to 12-pound turkey*
1 recipe Dry Cornbread,
    following
4 slices stale white bread,
    toasted and crumbled
1 cup coarsely chopped pecans
¼ cup minced fresh parsley
1 tablespoon fresh thyme
1 teaspoon minced fresh sage
¼ pound sweet butter
1 medium-size onion, chopped
3 ribs celery, chopped
1 small green bell pepper,
    seeded and chopped
1 bunch green onions,
    chopped
1 cup fresh corn kernels (2 to 3
    ears)
½ cup turkey or chicken stock
24 large fresh oysters,
    shucked, liquor reserved
2 eggs, lightly beaten
Salt and pepper to taste

Preheat oven to 450°F. In a large mixing bowl, toss together cornbread, crumbled toast, pecans, parsley, thyme and sage. In a large skillet melt half the butter. Add onion, celery, bell pepper and green onions. Cook over moderate heat, stirring until tender, about 10 minutes; do not brown. Add corn and cook 2 to 3 more minutes. Set aside.

In a small saucepan combine stock, ½ cup of reserved oyster liquor and remaining butter. Heat together until butter is melted. Mix pecans, parsley, thyme and sage with corn-bread mixture. Stir in cooked vegetables, stock mixture and eggs. Add salt and pepper. Gently fold in oysters.

SUGGESTED OYSTERS    Blue-point or Chincoteague.

## DRY CORNBREAD

1 cup all-purpose flour
3 teaspoons baking powder
1 teaspoon salt
2 tablespoons sugar
1 cup yellow cornmeal
2 eggs
1 cup milk
¼ cup vegetable oil

Preheat oven to 400°F. Mix together flour, baking powder, salt, sugar and cornmeal; combine well. Gradually beat in eggs and milk until dry ingredients are well moistened. Stir in vegetable oil. Grease an 8 × 8-inch baking pan with additional vegetable oil and pour in batter. Bake 30 minutes, until the top is slightly brown.

## LIGHT FISH STOCK

A freshly made fish stock will make the recipes in this book taste better. If you're in a hurry, you can substitute 1 cup (8 ounces) clam juice and ½ cup water for 1½ cups fish stock.

*Makes three and one-half cups*
2 tablespoons butter
1 small onion, coarsely
    chopped
2 ribs celery, coarsely chopped
1 bay leaf
2 pounds bones from any
    white fish
4 cups water
1 cup dry white wine
Juice of 1 lemon

Melt butter in a 4-quart saucepan over medium heat. Add onion and celery. Sauté gently, stirring and tossing to avoid browning. Add bay leaf and fish bones; stir to combine. Add 2 cups of the water; bring to a quick boil. Reduce heat to simmer and add the other 2 cups of water, wine and lemon juice. Simmer 20 minutes, strain to remove bones and vegetables.

# Index

## INDEX TO RECIPES

A CONNOISSEUR'S
GUIDE TO OYSTERS
Use this legend to iden-
tify oysters in the photo-
graph on pages 46 and 47.

1. Portuguese
2. Yaquina Bay
3. Yaquina Bay
4. Wescott Bay
5. Preston Point
6. Small Portuguese
7. Portuguese
8. Quilcene
9. Willapa Bay
10. Hog Island
11. Kumamoto
12. Malpeque
13. Bluepoint
14. Small Malpeque
15. Apalachicola
16. Black Bay
17. Olympia
18. Belon

## PACIFIC HEIGHTS BAR & GRILL

Chef Lonnie Williams has presided over the kitchen at Pacific Heights Bar & Grill since the restaurant first opened its doors in November of 1984. A graduate of the California Culinary Academy, Williams has created an exciting seafood menu that reflects the best in the new American cooking. Under his direction the restaurant has won the praises of both the critics and the public. Orville Schell of *California Magazine* said of the restaurant, "the best seafood this side of a sandbar" and the *Zagat Restaurant Survey* named PHB&G in the top twenty-five most popular dining places in the Bay Area.

Pacific Heights Bar & Grill takes pride in its abundant oyster bar, one of the finest in the country. Featured daily are as many as twenty different types of oysters from Pacific, Atlantic and Gulf waters. *San Francisco Examiner* food writer Marjorie Rice called it, "one of the best-stocked oyster bars I've encountered." And it was named Best Bountiful Oyster Bar by *San Francisco Focus* magazine.

New customers at Pacific Heights Bar & Grill often ask if the fish is fresh. Williams has a newspaper clipping to prove it. In the *San Francisco Chronicle*, columnist Herb Caen wrote: "The fish aren't taking this lying down . . . Lonnie Williams, chef at PHB&G, reached into the refrigerator for a piece of fish and was bitten on the index finger by a quite live thirty-pound halibut." How fresh can you get?

Williams has teamed with Karen Warner—best-selling author and member of the San Francisco Professional Food Society—to write the first connoisseur's guide to oysters.